Collins
New Primary Maths

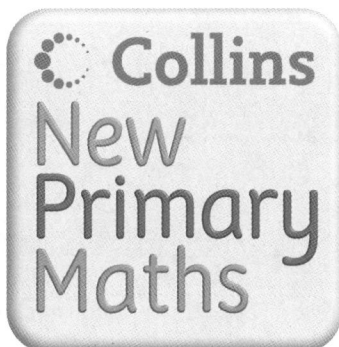

Homework Pack 2

Series Editor: Peter Clarke

Authors: Jo Power O'Keeffe, Jeanette Mumford, Andrew Edmondson

William Collins' dream of knowledge for all began with the publication of his first book in 1819. A self-educated mill worker, he not only enriched millions of lives, but also founded a flourishing publishing house. Today, staying true to this spirit, Collins books are packed with inspiration, innovation and practical expertise. They place you at the centre of a world of possibility and give you exactly what you need to explore it.

Collins. Freedom to teach.

Published by Collins
An imprint of HarperCollinsPublishers
77 – 85 Fulham Palace Road
Hammersmith
London
W6 8JB

Browse the complete Collins catalogue at
www.collinseducation.com

British Library Cataloguing in Publication Data
A Catalogue record for this publication is available from the British Library

Cover design by Laing&Carroll
Cover artwork by Jonatronix Ltd
Internal design by Steve Evans and Mark Walker Design
Illustrations by Steve Evans and Mark Walker
Edited by Jean Rustean
Proofread by Amanda Whyte

Printed and bound by Martins the Printers, Berwick-upon-Tweed

Contents

Unit C3

Unit D3

Unit E3

Name _____ Date _____

Two-digit daisies

- Know what each digit in a number less than 100 stands for

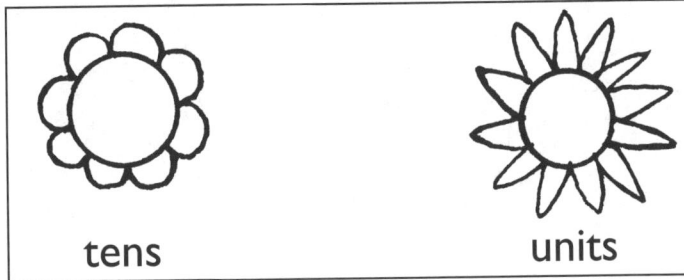

tens   units

5 1

51

3 6

4 3

9 2

1 7

4 5

1 2

5 3

9 4

What to do

Using the key at the top of the page, write the number represented by each flower in the pot in the space provided.
On the back: Write each number in words.

Name _____ Date _____

Sea sequences

● **Order two-digit numbers**

10 12 14 ○ ○ ○ 22

15 16 17 ○ 19 ○ 21

15 20 25 ○ ○ ○ 45

40 50 ○ ○ 80 ○ 100

11 13 15 ○ 19 ○ 23

14 24 34 ○ ○ ○ 74

What to do
Look carefully at each number sequence, and complete each one, writing in the missing numbers.
On the back: Choose any two-digit number between 10 and 30. Then write out the number patterns counting in 2s, 5s and 10s from your number up to 100.

Name _____ Date _____

Cake shop calculations

● **Solve problems involving money**

Emma bought…

5p and 9p

She used these coins

Theo bought…

9p and 9p

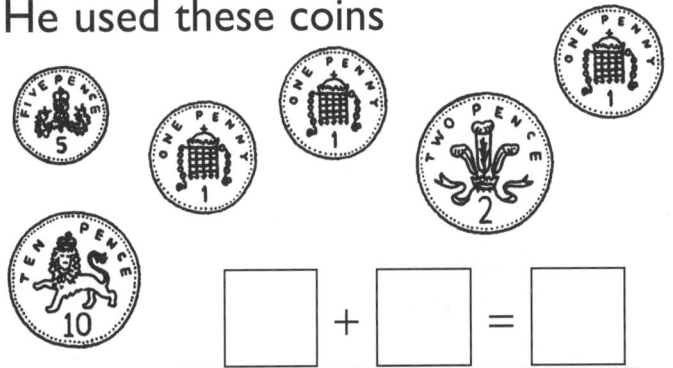

He used these coins

5 + □ = □

□ + □ = □

Sam bought…

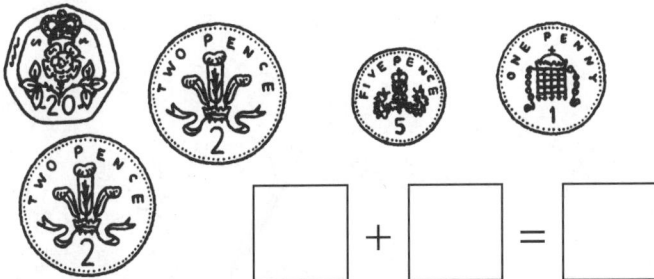

11p and 14p

He used these coins

□ + □ = □

Sara bought…

5p and 17p

She used these coins

□ + □ = □

Who spent the most money? _____

Who spent the least money? _____

How much change would Sam get from 30p? _____

How much change would Theo get from 20p? _____

© HarperCollinsPublishers Ltd 2008

What to do
Read each word problem. Colour in the coins each person uses to buy their two cakes.
Then, complete the calculation, and answer the questions.

Name _____ Date _____

How many beads?

● **Estimate a group of objects**

I estimate ☐ beads.

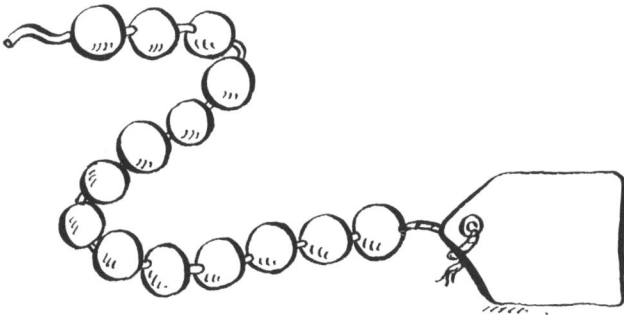

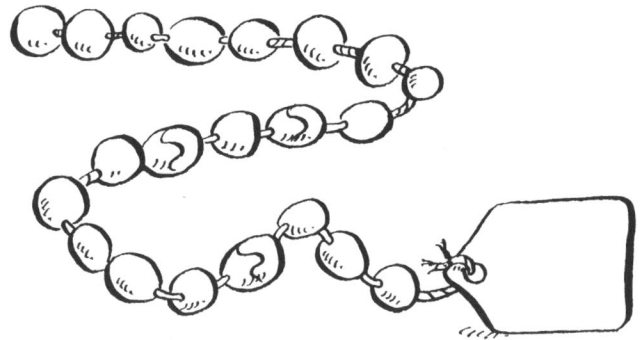

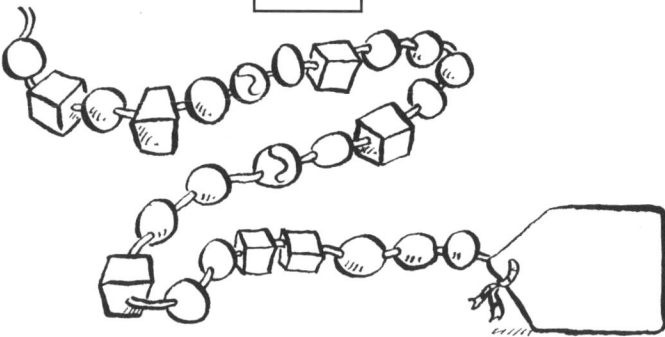

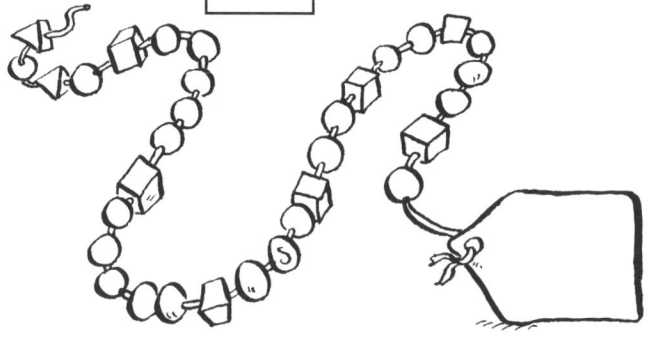

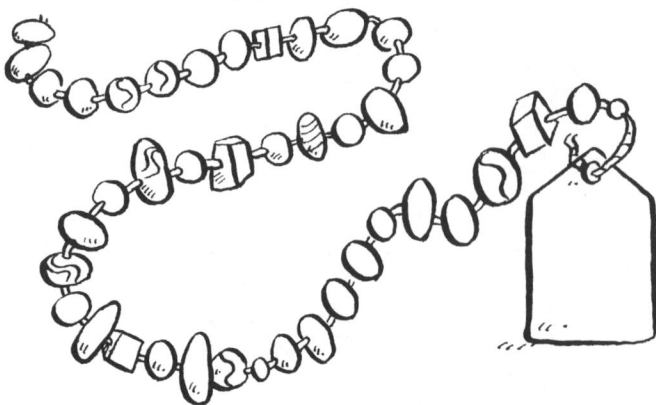

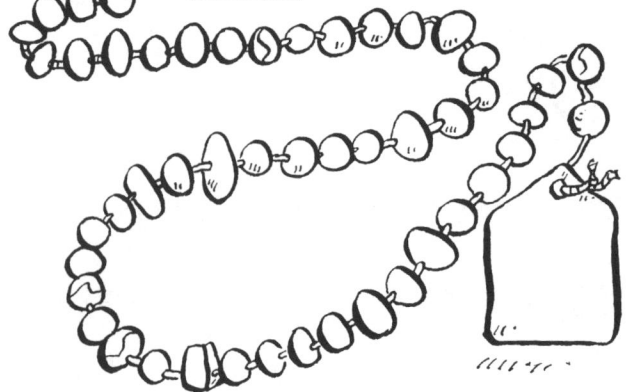

I estimate ☐ beads.

I estimate ☐ beads.

I estimate ☐ beads.

I estimate ☐ beads.

I estimate ☐ beads.

What to do

Estimate how many beads there are on each string and write it in the box. Then count the number of beads on each string and write it on the label. *On the back:* Use objects around the house to estimate. Take a handful of buttons, lego bricks or pencils and estimate how many you are holding. Then count them to check

Name _____ Date _____

Addition and subtraction facts

● **Know addition and subtraction facts for numbers to 10**

$2 - 1 =$ ☐

$4 - $ ☐ $= 2$

$4 - 3 =$ ☐

$5 - $ ☐ $= 3$

$5 - 1 =$ ☐

$6 - 3 =$ ☐

$6 - $ ☐ $= 2$

$7 - 4 =$ ☐

$7 - $ ☐ $= 2$

$8 - 6 =$ ☐

$8 - $ ☐ $= 4$

$9 - 1 =$ ☐

$9 - $ ☐ $= 6$

$10 - 7 =$ ☐

$10 - $ ☐ $= 2$

$4 + 1 =$ ☐

$2 + $ ☐ $= 5$

$3 + 3 =$ ☐

$5 + $ ☐ $= 6$

$4 + 3 =$ ☐

$5 + $ ☐ $= 7$

$3 + 5 =$ ☐

$4 + $ ☐ $= 8$

$9 + 0 =$ ☐

$7 + $ ☐ $= 9$

$6 + 4 =$ ☐

$5 + $ ☐ $= 10$

What to do
Find the missing numbers to complete the subtraction and addition calculations.

Name _____ Date _____

Paint pot addition

● **Use knowledge of number facts and operations**

Make up your own addition number sentences with the brushes and paint pots. Remember to put the larger number first!

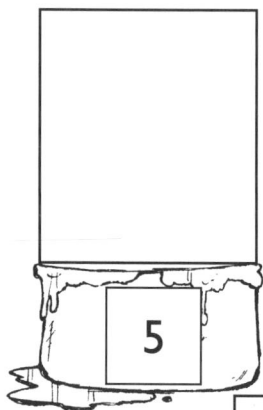

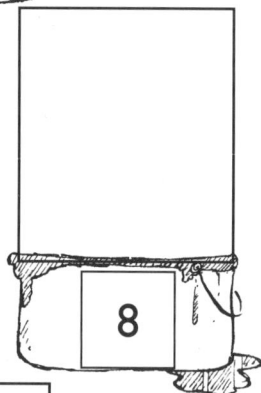

5

3

8

7

4

10

☐ + ☐ = ☐

☐ + ☐ = ☐

☐ + ☐ = ☐

☐ + ☐ = ☐

☐ + ☐ = ☐

☐ + ☐ = ☐

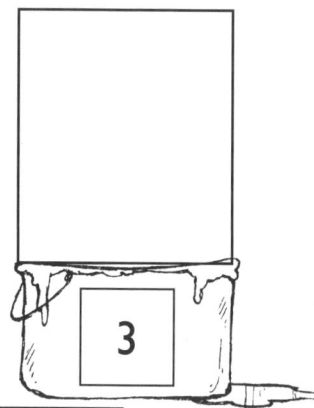

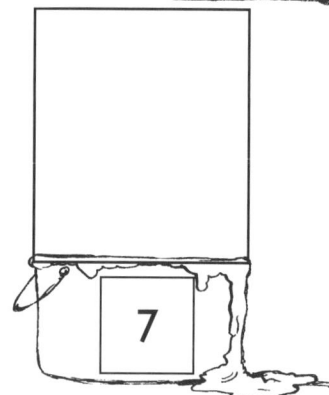

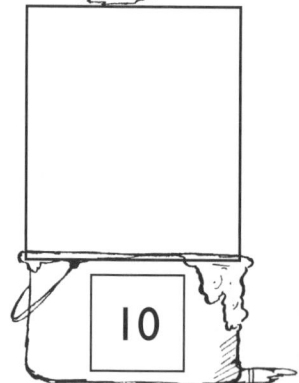

You need:
● scissors
● glue

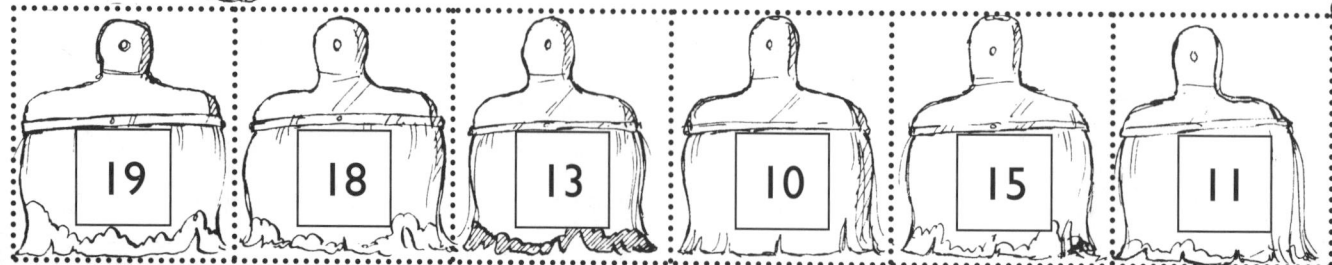

19   18   13   10   15   11

What to do

Create your own addition number sentences. Cut out the brushes at the bottom of the sheet and stick each brush with a paint pot. Write the numbers on the brush and point pot in the spaces provided to make an addition calculation and complete it by filling in the answer.

Name _____ Date _____

How much?

● **Solve problems involving money**

You need:
● scissors
● glue

£1.12

£2.30	£1.28	£3.52	£1.49	£1.25	£2.32

What to do

Look at the money in each pair of money bags and work out how much is in each one. Write this amount on the label attached to the bag. Cut the priced items from the bottom of the sheet. Then work out the total amount of money in each pair and match the bags to the item showing this amount to see who buys what.

Name _____ Date _____

Training by numbers

● **Describe patterns and relationships**

You need:

● red and blue coloured pencils

$\triangle + \triangle = 6$

$\bigcirc + \triangle = 9$

$\bigcirc + \bigcirc = 10$

$\triangle + \bigcirc + \triangle = 12$

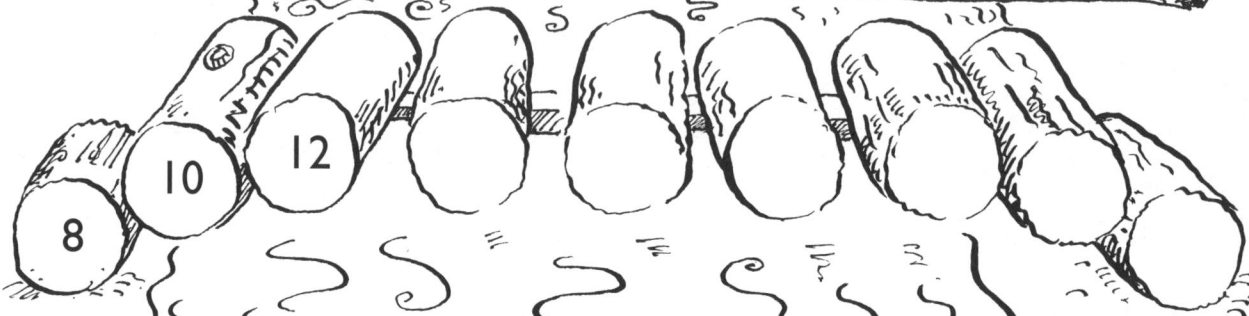

Side numbers (top to bottom): 19, ◯, 15, ◯, 11, ◯, ◯, ◯

Plank circles: 5, 7, 9, ◯, ◯, ◯, ◯

Logs: 8, 10, 12

Stones: 13, 2, 20, 15, 16, 24, 27, 11, 4, 3, 30, 5, 17, 6, 31, 7, 28, 14, 29, 13, 8, 10

What to do

Top: Write odd numbers in the triangles △ and even numbers in the circles ◯ to make the total.

Side and middle: Continue the number sequences.

Bottom: Colour the odd numbers red and the even numbers blue.

Name _____ Date _____

Pentagons, hexagons and octagons

● **Recognise 2-D shapes**

You need:

● coloured pencils

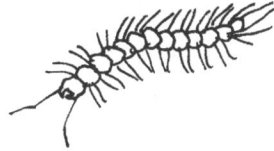

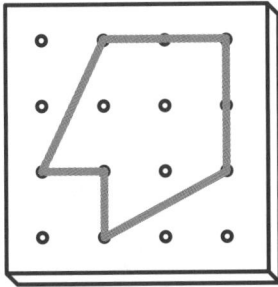

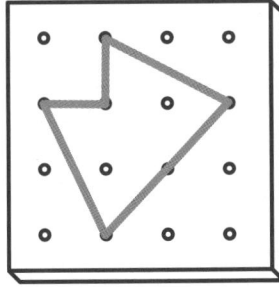

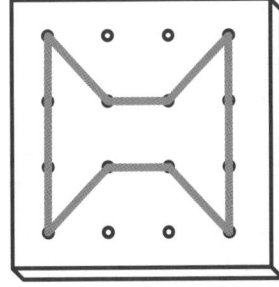

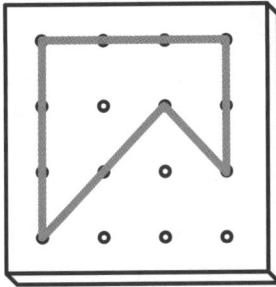

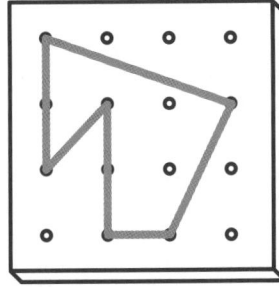

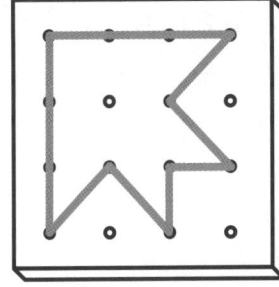

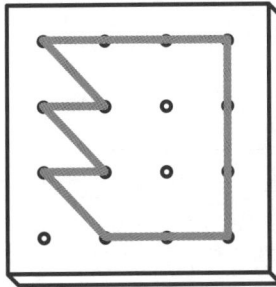

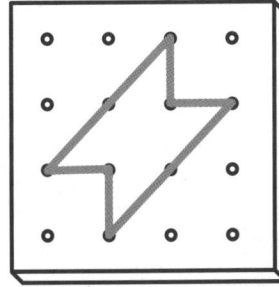

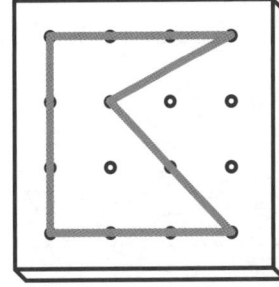

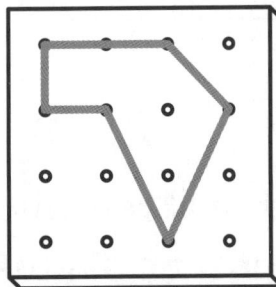

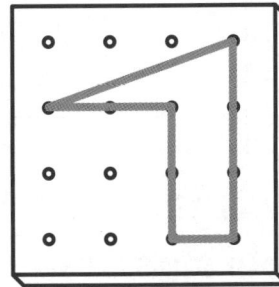

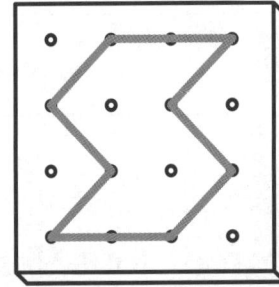

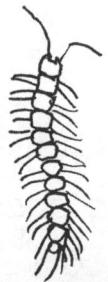

What to do

Count the number of sides for each shape. Colour all the shapes with the same number of sides the same colour.

Name _____ Date _____

Kitchen containers

● **Predict the shape of the base of a 3-D solid and whether or not it will roll**

1 Find containers in your kitchen for each of these bases.

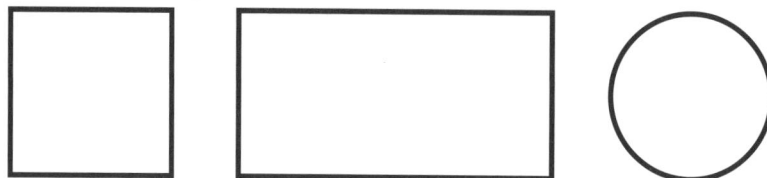

Tick the column which matches the base of your container.

Container	Shape of base			Will slide	Will roll
	☐	▭	◯		
Bottle of water			✔		
Box of					
Tin of					
Bottle of					
Carton of					
Jar of					
of					
of					

2 Guess which containers will slide and which will roll when placed on a slope. Test your guesses and put a tick in the correct column.

What to do

Find some packets, boxes, tins, jars and bottles in your kitchen which have different bases. Complete the table for the base of each item. Prop up an object like a chopping board to make a slope. Test whether each container will roll or slide and mark the result with a tick.

Name _____ Date _____

At home with centimetres

● **Estimate, measure and compare lengths using centimetres**

Find and measure these objects in your home.

[ ] cm long   [ ] cm wide   [ ] cm tall

Choose three more things to measure in centimetres.

Draw each object.

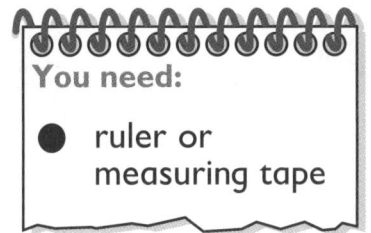

You need:
● ruler or measuring tape

Write how tall, long or wide it is.

[ ] cm   [ ]   [ ] cm   [ ]   [ ] cm

What to do
Use a ruler or measuring tape to find out how long, wide or tall things are in your home to the nearest centimetre.

Name _____ Date _____

Organising key rings

● **Put information in a table**

Count the keys on
each key ring.

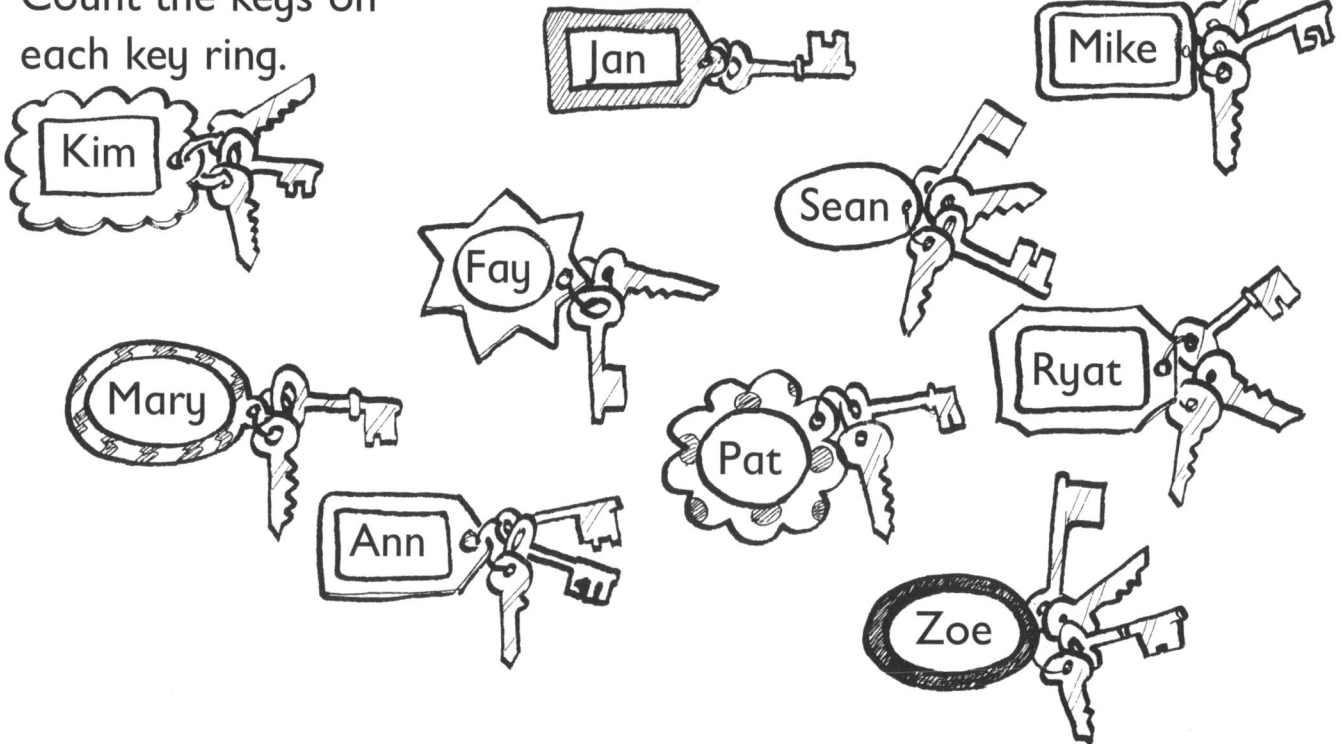

Kim

Jan

Mike

Fay

Sean

Mary

Ryat

Pat

Ann

Zoe

Write the names in the table. Write the totals in the boxes.

1 key	2 keys	3 keys	4 keys

How many key rings have 3 keys?

How many key rings have 1 or 2 keys?

Which number of keys is most common?

© HarperCollinsPublishers Ltd 2008

What to do

Count the keys on each key ring and write the names in the table. Write the total number of key rings in each column in the box. Then answer the questions below.

Name _____ Date _____

Sorting objects by length

● Sort objects and use diagrams to show how they were sorted

Shorter than arrow	Larger than arrow

☐

☐ objects are longer than the arrow.

☐ objects are shorter than the arrow.

Shorter than half arrow	Between half and whole arrow	Longer than arrow

☐ objects are shorter than half the arrow.

☐ objects are longer than the half arrow but shorter than the whole arrow.

☐ objects are **not** shorter than the arrow.

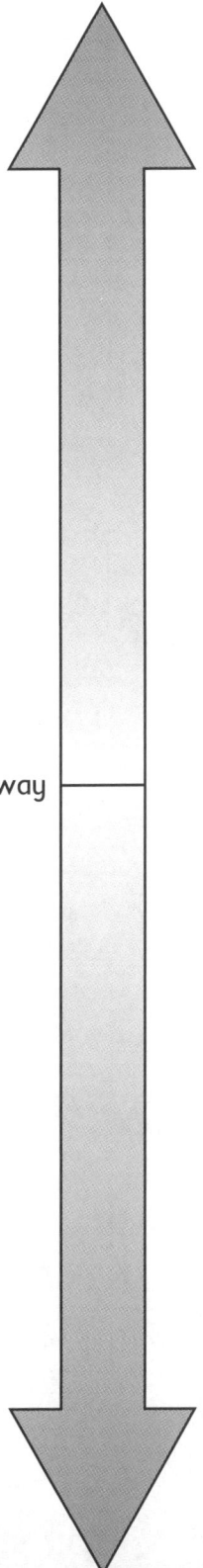

Halfway

© HarperCollinsPublishers Ltd 2008

What to do

Find 10 different objects in your bedroom. Compare their lengths with the arrow. Write their names in the top sets. Count the objects in each set and write the number in the box. Complete the sentences. Repeat for the bottom sets and sentences.

Name _____ Date _____

Fruit assortment

● **Put information in a table**

apple	orange	banana

[ ] people chose apple as their favourite fruit.

The most popular fruit is [   ].

Can eat the skin	Cannot eat the skin

You can eat the skins of [ ] fruit.

What to do
Ask friends and family which fruit they prefer. Make a tick for each person. Count the ticks and complete the table and sentences. Use the bottom sets to sort fruits by their skins. Write down the names of as many fruits as you can. Count the fruits and write the numbers in the boxes. Complete the sentence.

Name _____ Date _____

Bridging through 10

● **Add any pair of one-digit numbers**

$7 + 6 =$ ☐

$8 + 4 =$ ☐

$9 + 5 =$ ☐

$3 + 8 =$ ☐

$4 + 9 =$ ☐

$5 + 8 =$ ☐

$6 + 9 =$ ☐

$7 + 4 =$ ☐

$5 + 6 =$ ☐

What to do
Solve the addition calculations by bridging through 10.
On the back: Work out these addition calculations and write the addition fact for 10 that you use for each
one: $7 + 8 =$ ☐, $8 + 9 =$ ☐, $9 + 7 =$ ☐.

Name _____ Date _____

Cauldron calculations

- Add and subtract a one-digit number to and from a 'tens' number

Maths Magician is making spells with multiples of 10!

30   10   20

+ 5

25   35   15

20   40   30

– 6

34   24   14

50   40   10

+ 7

47   17   57

30   50   40

– 8

32   22   42

What to do

Add or subtract the one-digit number on each cauldron to or from each multiple of 10 on the bubbles. Find the star that has the answer and colour the star and bubble to match.

On the back: Change the + to a – and the – to a + in each calculation and work out the answers on 2 of the cauldrons.

Name _____ Date _____

Cutlery counting

● **Solve problems involving length**

knife ☐ cm

fork ☐ cm

dessertspoon ☐ cm

teaspoon ☐ cm

You need:
● cutlery
● ruler

1 What different lengths can you make?

Place end to end:

A knife and a fork   ☐ cm altogether

A knife and a dessertspoon   ☐ cm altogether

A knife and a teaspoon   ☐ cm altogether

2 How much shorter is:

A teaspoon than a knife?   ☐ cm

A teaspoon than a fork?   ☐ cm

A teaspoon than a dessertspoon?   ☐ cm

What to do

Find four different pieces of cutlery: knife, fork, dessertspoon and teaspoon. Use a ruler to measure the length of each piece to the nearest centimetre and write it in the box. Then use your answers to solve the problems.

Name _____ Date _____

Timers

- **Use different timers**

Find 3 different timers in your home.

Write the names here.

1 [_____]

2 [_____]

3 [_____]

Draw one of the timers.

[ ]

Write about the timer.

We use the timer to

[ ]

It measures time in

[ ]

Think of something you can do several times in one minute.

Ask a grown-up to time you for one minute.

Write what you did.

[ ]

What to do

Find three different timers in your home, e.g. cooking timer, and answer the questions. If there are any difficulties then a watch or clock with a seconds sweep-hand can be used instead.

Name _____ Date _____

Space explorer sums

● Calculate the value of an unknown number

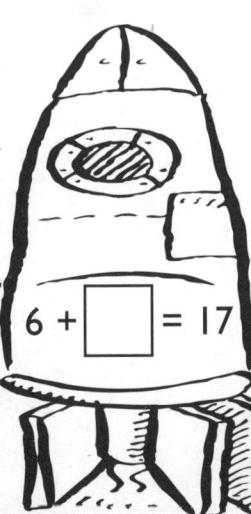

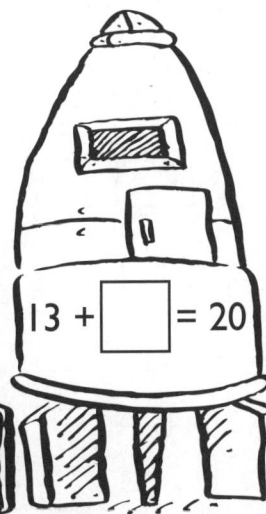

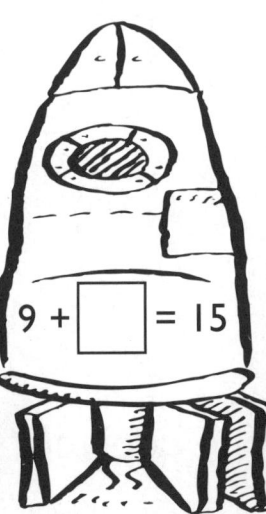

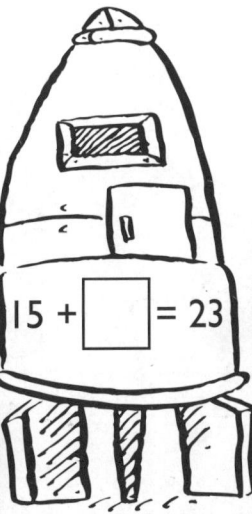

7

11

10

8

6

9

12

5

$6 +\ \square = 17$

$13 +\ \square = 20$

$9 +\ \square = 15$

$15 +\ \square = 23$

$12 +\ \square = 21$

What to do

Look at the calculation on each rocket and draw a line to match it to the planet showing the number that will complete it correctly.

On the back: There are 3 planets that a rocket has not landed on. Write an addition calculation for each one.

Halves and quarters

● Find one half and one quarter of shapes and sets of objects

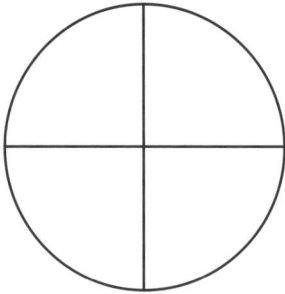

half

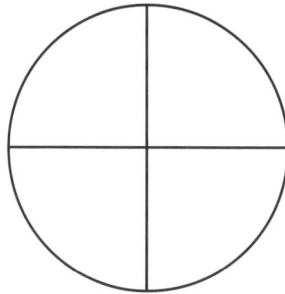

$\frac{1}{4}$

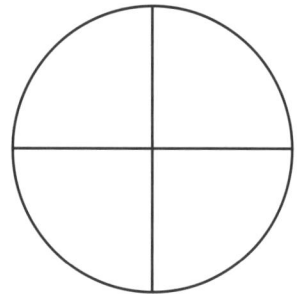

three quarters

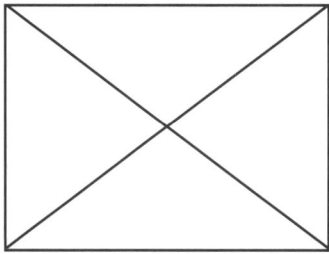

one quarter

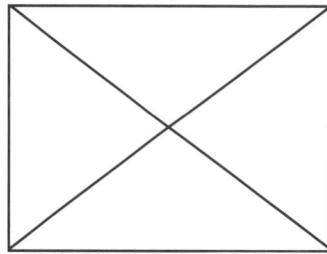

one whole

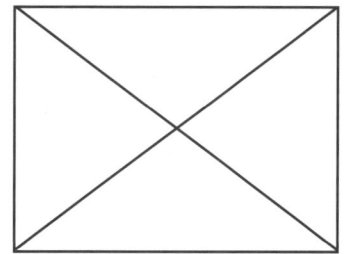

$\frac{1}{2}$

$\frac{1}{4}$

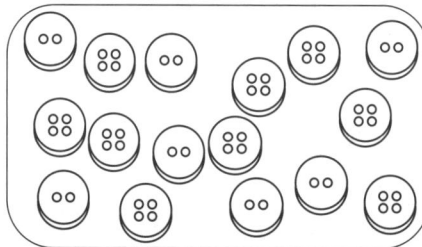

$\frac{1}{2}$

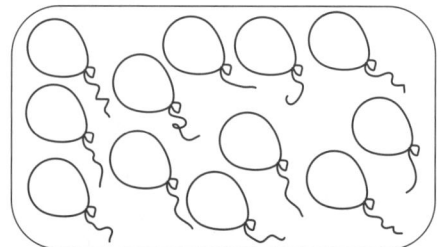

$\frac{1}{4}$

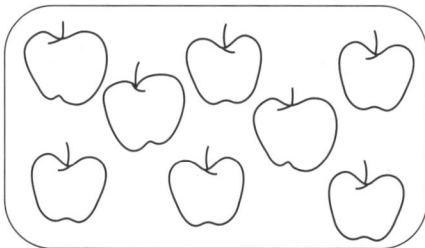

half

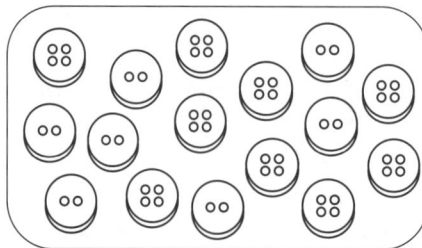

one quarter

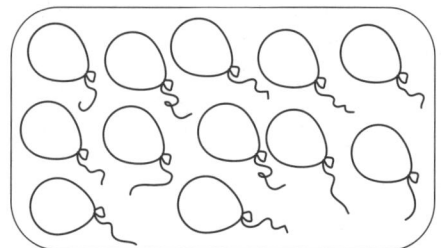

$\frac{1}{2}$

What to do

In each row, colour each shape or set of objects according to the fraction shown.

Name _____ Date _____

Multiplying by 2

● **Represent repeated addition as multiplication; use the 'x' symbol**

You need:
● scissors
● glue

$1 \times 2 =$ 2

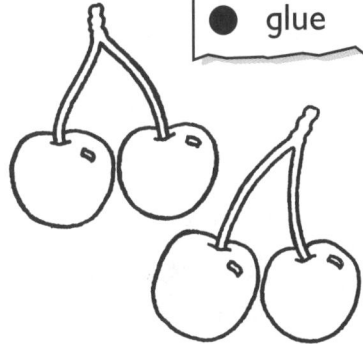

$10 \times 2 =$ ☐ $1 \times 2 =$ ☐ $5 \times 2 =$ ☐

$4 \times 2 =$ ☐ $7 \times 2 =$ ☐ $2 \times 2 =$ ☐

What to do

Cut out the calculations from the bottom of the sheet. Match them to the appropriate cherries. Then complete each calculation.
On the back: Find the answers for these calculations and draw the cherries to match: $3 \times 2, 6 \times 2, 8 \times 2, 9 \times 2$.

Name _____ Date _____

Dividing by 2

● Use the ÷ and = symbols to record number sentences

☐ = 2	☐ = ☐	☐ = ☐

☐ = ☐	☐ = ☐	☐ = ☐

14 ÷ 2	4 ÷ 2	10 ÷ 2
6 ÷ 2	12 ÷ 2	8 ÷ 2

You need:
● scissors
● glue

What to do
Cut out the calculations from the bottom of the sheet. Match them to the appropriate picture. Then complete each calculation.
On the back: Write and complete these number sentences, drawing spotty balloons to match: 16 ÷ 2, 18 ÷ 2, 20 ÷ 2.

Name _____ Date _____

Multiplication time

● **Know the 2, 5 and 10 times tables**

$1 \times 2 =$ ☐	$1 \times 10 =$ ☐	$1 \times 5 =$ ☐
$4 \times 2 =$ ☐	$4 \times 10 =$ ☐	$4 \times 5 =$ ☐
$3 \times 2 =$ ☐	$3 \times 10 =$ ☐	$3 \times 5 =$ ☐
$5 \times 2 =$ ☐	$5 \times 10 =$ ☐	$5 \times 5 =$ ☐
$2 \times 2 =$ ☐	$2 \times 10 =$ ☐	$2 \times 5 =$ ☐
$8 \times 2 =$ ☐	$8 \times 10 =$ ☐	$8 \times 5 =$ ☐
$6 \times 2 =$ ☐	$6 \times 10 =$ ☐	$6 \times 5 =$ ☐
$10 \times 2 =$ ☐	$10 \times 10 =$ ☐	$10 \times 5 =$ ☐
$7 \times 2 =$ ☐	$7 \times 10 =$ ☐	$7 \times 5 =$ ☐
$9 \times 2 =$ ☐	$9 \times 10 =$ ☐	$9 \times 5 =$ ☐

What to do

Complete each of the multiplication facts for 2, 5 and 10 and write the answers in the spaces provided.
On the back: Multiply 2, 5 and 10 by each of the numbers from 11 to 15 and write down each calculation.

Name _____ Date _____

Juggling problems

● **Know the 2, 5 and 10 multiplication and division facts**

$\boxed{1} \times \boxed{2} = \boxed{}$

$\boxed{} \div \boxed{} = \boxed{}$

$\boxed{} \times \boxed{} = \boxed{}$

$\boxed{} \div \boxed{} = \boxed{}$

$\boxed{} \times \boxed{} = \boxed{}$

$\boxed{} \div \boxed{} = \boxed{}$

$\boxed{} \times \boxed{} = \boxed{}$

$\boxed{} \div \boxed{} = \boxed{}$

What to do

Look at the three numbers in each panel. The numbers make one division and one multiplication calculation. Rearrange the numbers and write the calculations in the spaces provided.

Name _____ Date _____

Footsteps

- Describe and extend simple number patterns

Count on in steps.

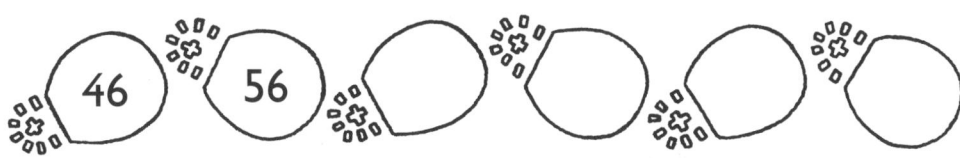

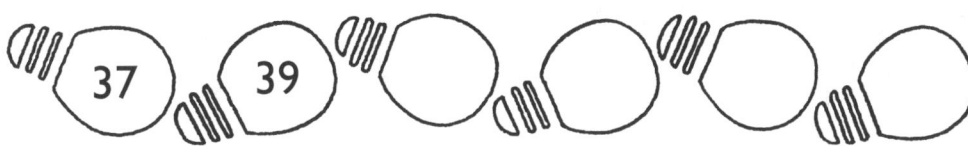

26 27 28 29 30 31 | 1 |

3 8 13

46 56

37 39

Count back in steps.

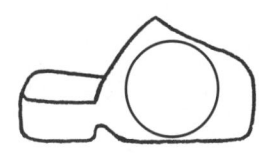

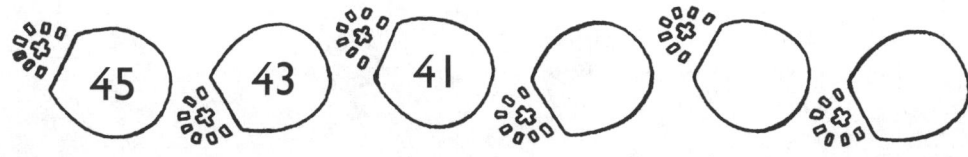

48 46 44

32 27 22

60 50 40

45 43 41

What to do

Fill in the missing numbers in the footprints. Write the appropriate step on the boots.
On the back: Make up your own number patterns by choosing an odd and an even number
between 30 and 60 and counting on and back in 2s, 5s and 10s.

Name _____ Date _____

Number name nests

● **Read and write two-digit numbers in figures and words**

You need:
● scissors
● glue

forty two

sixty eight

fifty one

ninety nine

seventy four

4	3	9	6	4	1
8	2	7	5	9	5

© HarperCollins*Publishers* Ltd 2008

What to do

Look at the number name on each nest. Cut out the digits from the bottom of this sheet and match them to the nests.
On the back: Use the two digits that are left to make two more two-digit numbers. Draw a nest for each one and write the number name underneath.

Name _____ Date _____

Tens and Units teasers

● **Add and subtract pairs of two-digit numbers**

14 + 15   20 + 14   32 + 13

14 (+) 15 (=) 29   □ ○ □ ○ □   □ ○ □ ○ □

27 (−) 13 (=) 14   36 (−) 21 (=) □   49 (−) 32 (=) □

What to do

Top: Draw a line to match each number to the tens or units tent. Draw the spots on the tent to represent the tens and units. Then complete the addition calculation underneath.

Bottom: Cross out the number of spots that are to be taken away. Calculate the number left to complete the calculation.

Racing addition and subtraction

● **Calculate the value of an unknown in a number sentence**

$15 + 3 = \boxed{}$

$12 + \boxed{} = 17$

$\boxed{} + 4 = 13$

$12 + \boxed{} = 16$

$17 + 8 = \boxed{}$

$\boxed{} + 6 = 29$

$16 - 2 = \boxed{}$

$\boxed{} - 10 = 1$

$18 - \boxed{} = 3$

$\boxed{} - 5 = 6$

$20 - 14 = \boxed{}$

$15 - \boxed{} = 9$

The wheels are near doubles.
Work them out using a double.

$\boxed{6} + \boxed{6} + 1 = \boxed{13}$ 6   7

$\boxed{} + \boxed{} + 1 = \boxed{}$ 4   5

$\boxed{} + \boxed{} - 1 = \boxed{}$ 9   8

0 1 2 3 4 5 6 7 8 9 10 11 12 13 14 15 16 17 18 19 20 21 22 23 24 25 26 27 28 29 30

What to do

Complete the calculations. Use the number line to help.
On the back: Write as many different additions and subtractions as you can using the numbers 1, 2, 3, 4, 5. Work them out.

Name _____ Date _____

Totals for 10, 20 and 100

● Know pairs with a total of 10 and 20, and pairs of
multiples of 10 that total 100

6 + 4

15 + 5

10

100

11 + 9

3 + 7

100

10

90 + 10

20 + 80

20

100

40 + 60

30 + 70

20

100

What to do

Match the calculation on each pirate to the treasure chest showing the correct answer.

On the back: Write down 10 different addition calculations for totals of 10, 20 and 100

Name _____ Date _____

Monster multiples

● **Know multiplication facts for the 2, 5 and 10 times tables**

Column 1

1 × 2 = ☐

2 × ☐ = 4

☐ × 2 = 6

4 × 2 = ☐

5 × 2 = ☐

6 × ☐ = 12

7 × 2 = ☐

8 × ☐ = 16

☐ × 2 = 18

10 × 2 = ☐

Column 2

1 × 5 = ☐

2 × 5 = ☐

3 × ☐ = 15

☐ × 5 = 20

5 × 5 = ☐

6 × ☐ = 30

☐ × 5 = 35

8 × ☐ = 40

☐ × 5 = 45

10 × 5 = ☐

Column 3

1 × 10 = ☐

2 × 10 = ☐

☐ × 10 = 30

4 × ☐ = 40

5 × 10 = ☐

☐ × 10 = 60

7 × ☐ = 70

8 × 10 = ☐

☐ × 10 = 90

10 × 10 = ☐

What to do

Complete each of the multiplication facts for the 2, 5 and 10 times tables.
On the back: Write the pattern of multiples for 2, 5 and 10. Can you continue each pattern to 100?

Name _____ Date _____

Library totals

- **Solve word problems**

There are 12 books on the top shelf. 3 books are removed.

☐ ⊖ ☐ ⊜ ☐

3 more are removed.

☐ ⊖ ☐ ⊜ ☐

5 books are put on the bottom shelf. How many books on the shelves altogether?

☐ ⊕ ☐ ⊜ ☐

There are ☐ books.

There are 4 books on the top shelf. 4 books are put on the bottom shelf.

☐ ⊕ ☐ ⊜ ☐

2 books are removed.

☐ ⊖ ☐ ⊜ ☐

10 books are put on the top shelf. How many books on the shelves altogether?

☐ ⊕ ☐ ⊜ ☐

There are ☐ books.

There are 16 books on the top shelf. 5 books are removed.

☐ ◯ ☐ ⊜ ☐

3 books are put on the top shelf.

☐ ◯ ☐ ⊜ ☐

5 books are put on the bottom shelf. How many books on the shelves altogether?

☐ ◯ ☐ ⊜ ☐

There are ☐ books.

There are 6 books on the top shelf. 4 books are put on the bottom shelf.

☐ ◯ ☐ ⊜ ☐

3 books are removed.

☐ ◯ ☐ ⊜ ☐

10 books are put on the top shelf. How many books on the shelves altogether?

☐ ◯ ☐ ⊜ ☐

There are ☐ books.

What to do

Write addition and subtraction calculations to find the total number of books on the shelves.

Name _____ Date _____

Comparing wagon numbers

● **Describe patterns and relationships involving numbers**

14 **5**

| □ is odd | □ is even |
| □ is bigger | □ is smaller |
| The difference is □ |

31 **16**

| □ is odd | □ is even |
| □ is bigger | □ is smaller |
| The difference is □ |

Write the numbers in order from smallest to largest.

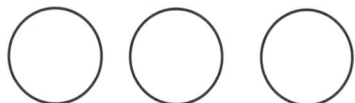

23 **8** **15**

○ ○ ○

Odd numbers □

Even numbers □

□ and □ are closest.

95 **22** **58**

○ ○ ○

Odd numbers □

Even numbers □

□ and □ are closest.

What to do

Top: Write the answers in the boxes underneath the trains.

Bottom: Order the numbers on the carriages and write the answers in the boxes underneath.

On the back: Look at these numbers: 27, 13, 6, 10, 5, 18, 28, 35, 50. Compare the numbers using the words above.

Name _____ Date _____

Dastardly digits

● Read and write two-digit and three-digit numbers in figures and words

86

117

30

134

41

221

🏁1 🏁4 🏁2

🏁5 🏁3 🏁6

You need:
● scissors
● glue

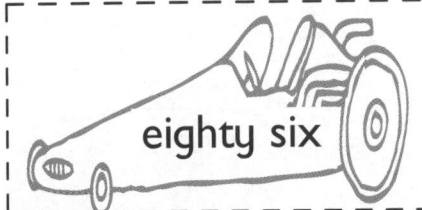

one hundred and seventeen

one hundred and thirty four

forty one

eighty six

thirty

two hundred and twenty one

What to do

Top: Cut out the racing cars from the bottom of the sheet and match them to the correct drivers.

Bottom: Look at the numbers on each set of three finishing flags. Make three different three-digit numbers from each set and write them in the spaces provided.

Name _____ Date _____

Symmetry in pictures

● **Draw a line of symmetry on a shape**

I found these pictures. I drew the line of symmetry on the sofa with a felt pen. Draw the line of symmetry on my other pictures. Do the same with your own pictures.

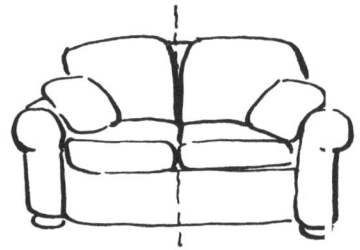

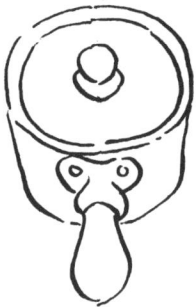

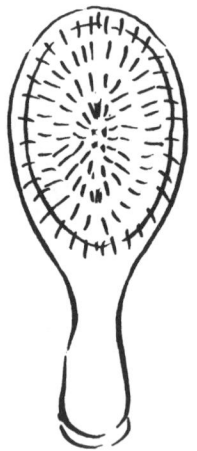

You need:
● ruler
● magazines or catalogues
● scissors
● glue

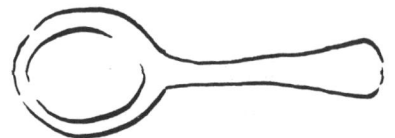

What to do

Look at the pictures and draw the line of symmetry through each of them. Using pictures from magazines or catalogues, discuss which ones show a line of symmetry. Draw the line of symmetry and cut out each picture and stick on this sheet.

Name _____ Date _____

What does it weigh?

● **Read numbers on a scale**

The [ ] is nearly [ ] kg heavy.

The [ ] is nearly [ ] kg heavy.

The [ ] is nearly [ ] kg heavy.

You need:

● kitchen or bathroom scales (or 1 kg bag of flour or sugar)

● 3 household items

● coloured pencils

What to do

Use kitchen or bathroom scales. Find three objects and weigh them. Draw a picture of each object and write its weight in the box. If no scales are available, compare the weight of your objects to a 1 kg bag of sugar or flour.

Name _____Date _____

Sorting faces

● **Sort objects and use diagrams to show how they are sorted**

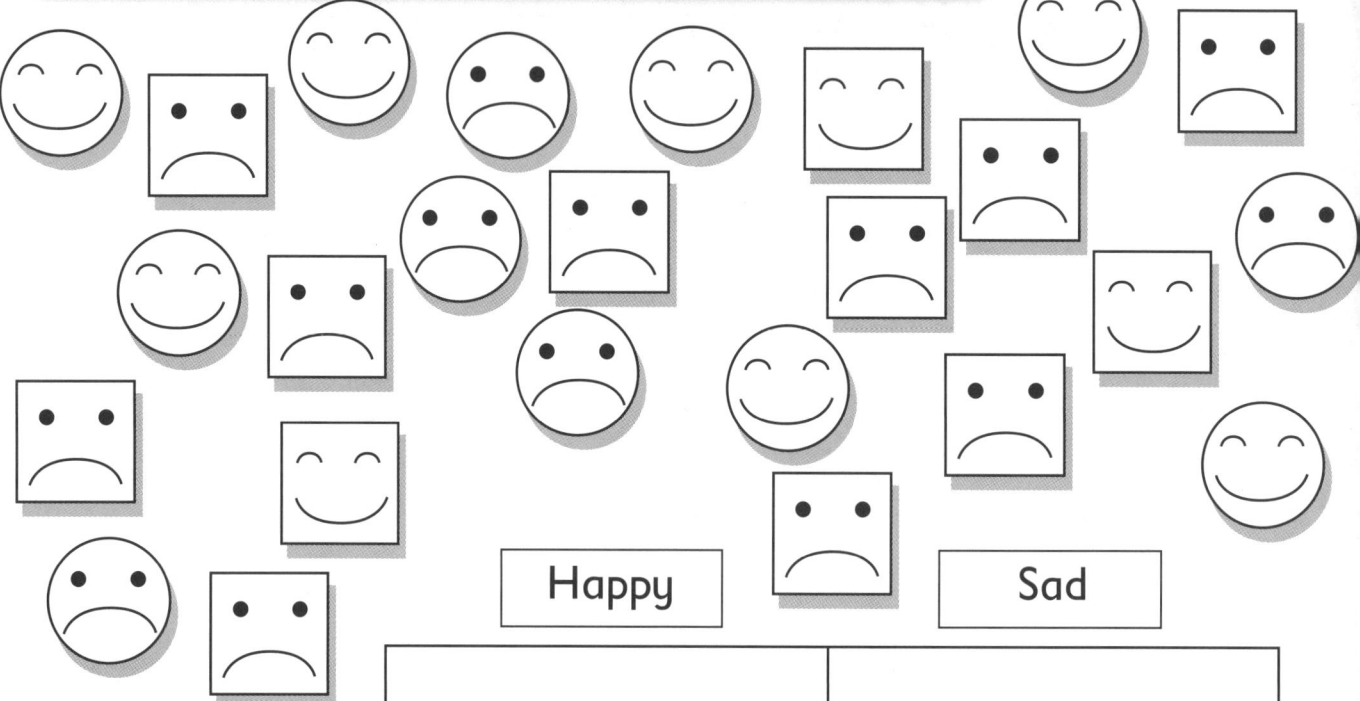

| Happy | | Sad |

| Round | | |
| Square | | |

There are [ ] happy square faces.   There are [ ] round faces.

There are [ ] round happy faces.   There are [ ] sad faces.

What to do
Copy each face into the correct set. Cross off the faces as you draw them. Count the faces and write the totals in the circles. Complete the sentences.

Name _____ Date _____

Favourite flavours

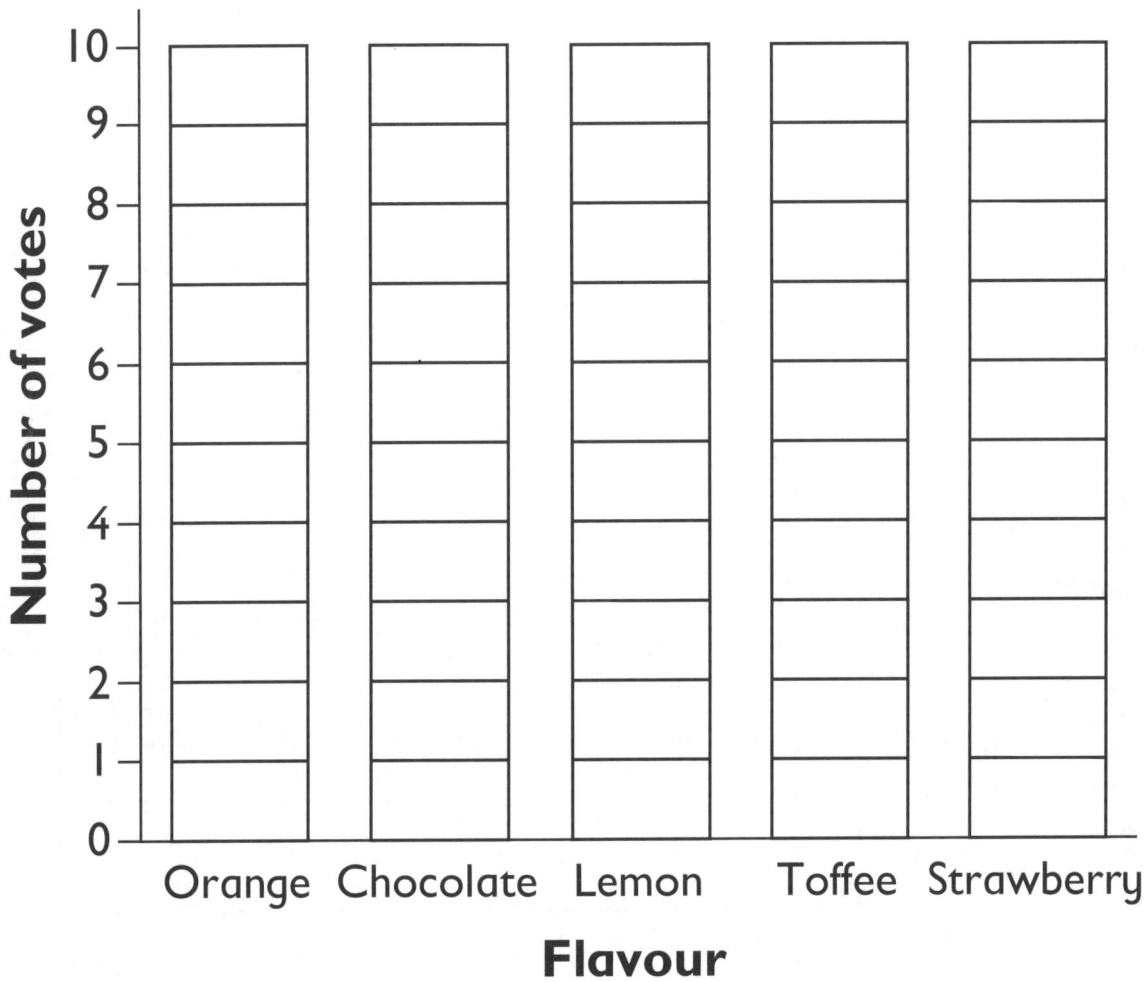

● **Make block graphs**

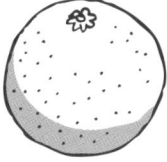

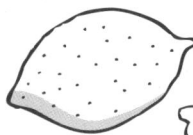

You need:
● coloured pencils

Favourite flavour

Number of votes

10					
9					
8					
7					
6					
5					
4					
3					
2					
1					
0	Orange	Chocolate	Lemon	Toffee	Strawberry

Flavour

The most popular flavour is [　　　　　　　　].

The least popular flavour is [　　　　　　　　].

What to do
Which flavour do you think people prefer? Ask your friends and family to vote for the flavour they prefer. Colour a block for each vote. Complete the block graph. Complete the sentences.

Name _____ Date _____

Travelling to work

● **Organise information and make block graphs**

How we travel to work

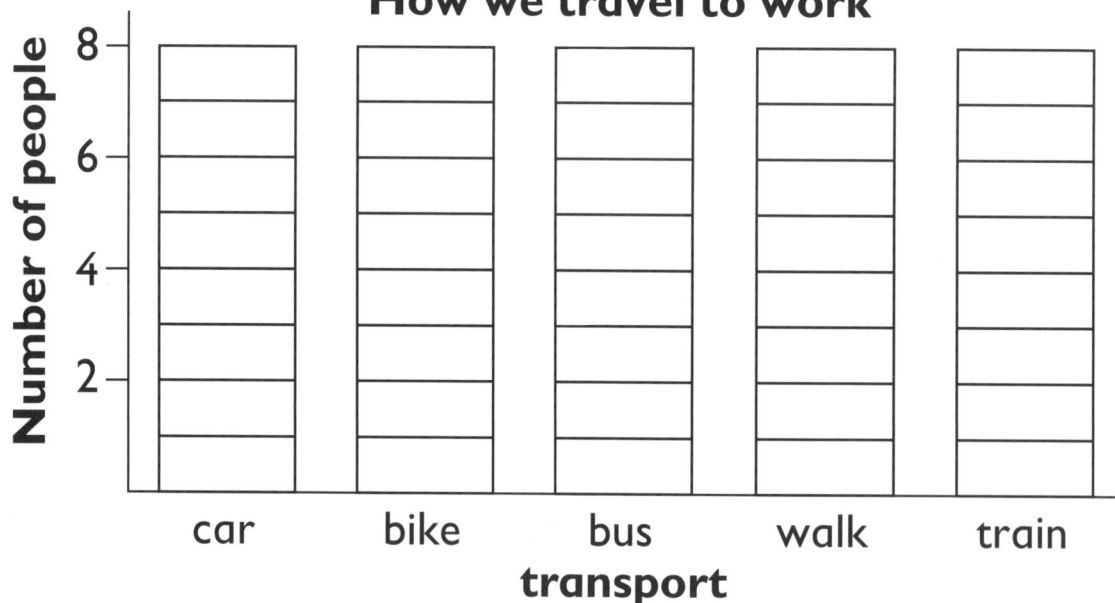

	by car	not by car
alone	◯	◯
not alone	◯	◯

How we travel to work

Number of people

8
6
4
2

car   bike   bus   walk   train

transport

[ ] is the most common way to travel to work.

[ ] people travel by car with someone else.

What to do
Ask people how they travel to work. Make a tick for each person in the correct set. Count the people and write the totals in the circles. Fill in a block for each person and complete the block graph. Complete the sentences.

Name _____ Date _____

Adding and subtracting bananas

● **Add and subtract mentally**

| 3 | $+$ | 2 | $=$ | 5 |
| 5 | $-$ | 2 | $=$ | 3 |

| | $+$ | | $=$ | |
| | $-$ | | $=$ | |

| | $+$ | | $=$ | |
| | $-$ | | $=$ | |

| | $+$ | | $=$ | |
| | $-$ | | $=$ | |

| | $+$ | | $=$ | |
| | $-$ | | $=$ | |

| | $+$ | | $=$ | |
| | $-$ | | $=$ | |

$$20 + 10 = 30$$

$$70 + 10 = \boxed{}$$

$$90 - 20 = \boxed{}$$

$$80 - 50 = \boxed{}$$

$$50 + \boxed{} = 100$$

$$70 + \boxed{} = 100$$

What to do

Top: Look at the bananas and write an addition and subtraction fact for each set to complete the calculations.
Bottom: Complete the calculations involving multiples of ten.
On the back: Write ten more addition facts. Write the subtraction facts that go with them.

Name _____ Date _____

Money box matching

● **Solve problems involving money**

Ben ☐

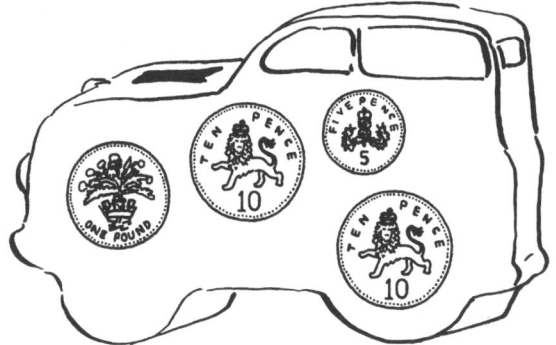

Erin ☐

Hassan ☐

Kaya ☐

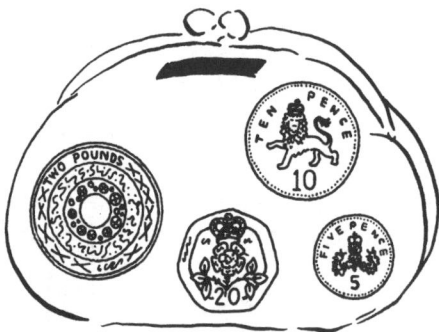

Luke ☐

Naomi ☐

You need:
● scissors
● glue

£1.25	£2.35	£2.30	£1.10	£2.40	£3.42

What to do

Look at the coins in each of the money boxes and calculate the amount in each. Cut out the correct amount from the bottom of the sheet and stick it underneath the appropriate money box.

Name _____ Date _____

Programme times

● **Solve a problem involving time**

Fire eater

I go on just before the gymnast.

I'm the last in the show.

Juggler

My act is half an hour after the trapeze artist

Ringmaster

Gymnast

My act comes just before the juggler.

Circus Programme

7:30   Clown _____

7:45   _____

8:00   _____

8:15   _____

8:30   _____

8:45   _____

9:00   _____

9:15   _____

Clown

I am the first at half past seven.

I go on at eight o'clock.

Trampoline act

I go on just before the trampoline act.

Trapeze artist

I come riding into the ring at half past eight.

Cyclist

What to do
Read each clue. Work out the starting time for each circus act and write it in the programme.

Name _____ Date _____

Half and quarter turns

● **Turn through whole, half and quarter turns**

Start	Quarter turn	Half turn

What to do

Draw each shape after a quarter and a half turn.

Name _____ Date _____

Mixed up monster multiplication

● **Understand multiplication**

| 0 | 1 | 2 | 3 | 4 | 5 | 6 | 7 | 8 | 9 | 10 | 11 | 12 | 13 | 14 | 15 | 16 | 17 | 18 | 19 | 20 | 21 | 22 | 23 | 24 | 25 |

3 × 2   12   6

2 × 5   4   4 × 2   4 × 3

20   1 × 4   10   8

5 × 5   16   4 × 5   15

3 × 3

4 × 4   25   9

3 × 5

What to do

Look at the calculations on each of the monsters. Draw a line to match each calculation to its correct answer, shown in a cave. If you need to, use the number track at the top of the sheet to help you.

Name _____ Date _____

Maths market day

● Solve word problems involving money

Lucy bought 5 flowers.
Each flower cost 3p.

☐ ⊗ ☐ = ☐ p.

Lucy spent ☐ p on flowers.

She bought a card for 4p.

☐ ⊕ ☐ = ☐ p.

Lucy spent ☐ p altogether.

HAPPY BIRTHDAY

Ellis spent 20p on stickers.
He bought 4 stickers.

☐ ÷ ☐ = ☐ p.

Each sticker cost ☐ p.

Ellis spent 20p on stickers and
15p on sweets.
How much did he spend?

☐ ⊕ ☐ = ☐ p.

Amir bought 4 cakes.
Each cake cost 7p.

☐ ○ ☐ ○ ☐ p.

Amir spent ☐ p on cakes.

Amir bought one more for his
Nan.

☐ ○ ☐ ○ ☐ p.

Altogether, Amir spent ☐ p
on cakes.

Min had 40p to spend.
She spent 4p on a lollypop.

☐ ○ ☐ ○ ☐ p.

Min had ☐ p left.

Min bought 5 pencils. Each pencil
cost 6p each.
How much did she spend?

☐ ○ ☐ ○ ☐ p.

Min spent ☐ p on pencils.

What to do
Solve each word problem using addition, subtraction, division or multiplication. Write out the
calculations for each problem, filling in the empty boxes with the correct numbers.
On the back: Make up one multiplication and one division word problem. Draw pictures for each one.

Name _____ Date _____

Multiplication missing numbers

● **Find a missing number in a number sentence**

You need:
● coloured pencils

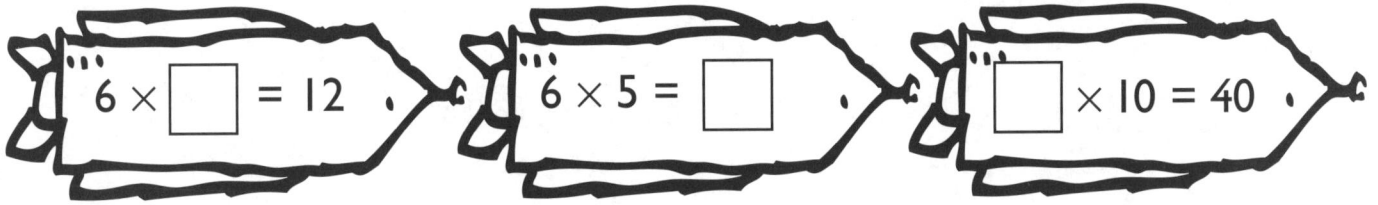

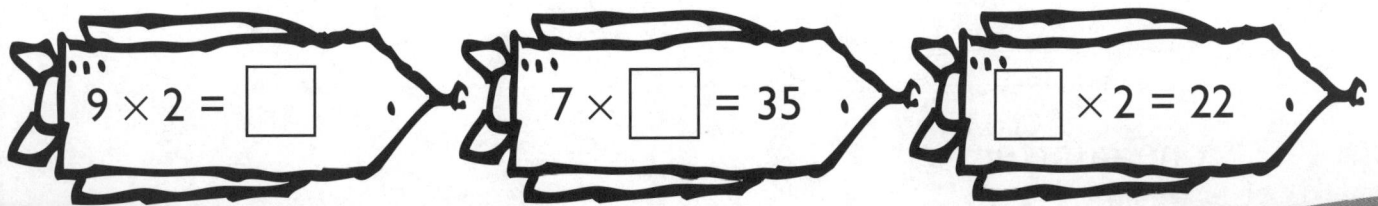

$6 \times \square = 12$

$6 \times 5 = \square$

$\square \times 10 = 40$

11

2

5

4

15

18

20

30

16

$9 \times 2 = \square$

$7 \times \square = 35$

$\square \times 2 = 22$

© HarperCollinsPublishers Ltd 2008

What to do

The stars show the answers to the multiplication number sentences on the rockets. Complete each number sentence to find which rocket reaches which star. Draw a line to join them, then colour them to match.

On the back: Make a multiplication calculation for the three stars that the rockets did not land on.

Name _____ Date _____

Quarters and halves

● Find one half, one quarter and three quarters of shapes
and sets of objects

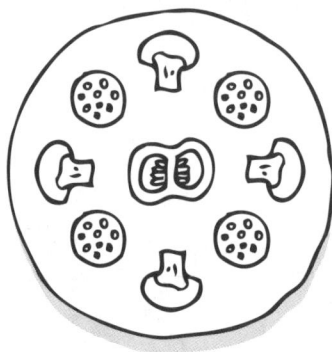

one half   one quarter $\frac{1}{4}$ $\frac{1}{2}$

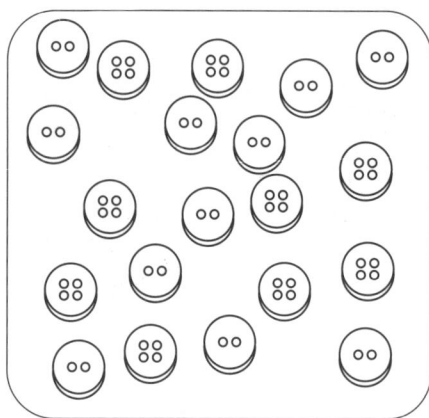

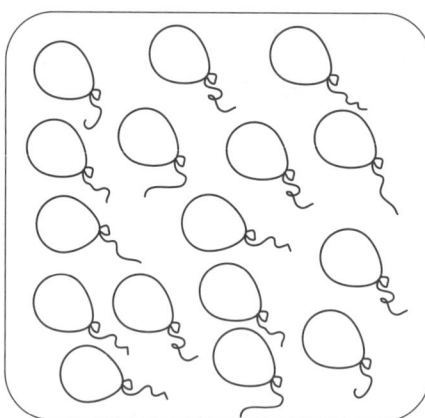

one half $\frac{1}{4}$ $\frac{1}{2}$

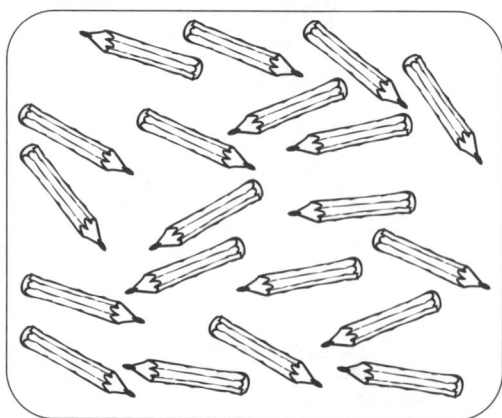

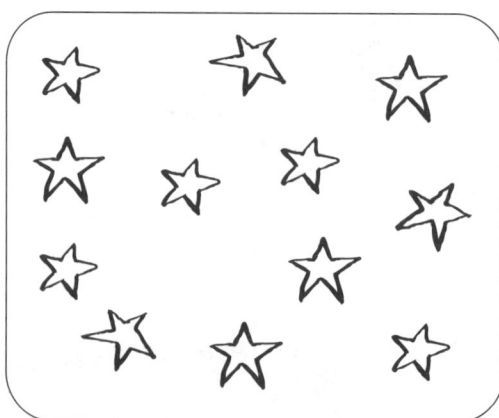

You need:

● coloured
pencils

one quarter $\frac{1}{2}$

What to do
Look at the words under each picture and colour each picture to match its' fraction.

Name _____ Date _____

Multi-storey multiplication

- ● **Know the 2, 5 and 10 times tables**
- ● **Recognise multiples of 2, 5 and 10**

2 × 2 =

5 × 2 =

7 × 2 =

1 × 2 =

3 × 2 =

6 × 2 =

4 × 2 =

8 × 2 =

3 × 10 =

6 × 10 =

2 × 10 =

7 × 10 =

5 × 10 =

9 × 10 =

4 × 10 =

8 × 10 =

2 × 5 =

4 × 5 =

1 × 5 =

3 × 5 =

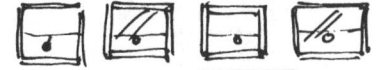

5 × 5 =

7 × 5 =

9 × 5 =

10 × 5 =

What to do

Complete each multiplication fact for 2, 5 and 10, writing the missing number in each calculation.
On the back: There are two missing multiplication facts for each block. Write them down and then write a division number sentence for each one.

Name _____ Date _____

Doubles and halves to 20

- Know doubles of all numbers to 20, and the matching halves

Double these numbers

| 4 | → | 8 |

| 8 | → | |

| 11 | → | |

| 15 | → | |

| 17 | → | |

| 20 | → | |

Halve these numbers

| 18 | → | |

| 10 | → | |

| 16 | → | |

| 12 | → | |

| 8 | → | |

| 14 | → | |

| 1 | 2 | 3 | | 5 | 6 | | 8 | 9 | 10 | 11 | 12 | | 14 | 15 | 16 | 17 | 18 | 19 | 20 |

| 2 | 4 | 6 | 8 | | | 14 | 16 | | 20 | | 24 | 26 | | 30 | | 34 | | 38 | |

What to do

Top: Double or half the numbers shown.

Bottom: Complete the number sequence.

On the back: Can you find the doubles of numbers from 21 to 25? How did you work it out?

Name _____ Date _____

Hammer steps

● **Count on and back in steps**

Count on or back in steps.
Write the numbers.

step 5

((7)

step 2

(31)

step 3

(26)

step 4

(13)

Find the step.
Write the missing numbers.

step

(5) (8) ( ) ( ) ( ) ( )

step

( ) (7) (11) ( ) ( ) ( )

step

( ) ( ) ( ) ( ) (26) (31)

What to do
Top: Use the step number written on the hammer to count on or back.
Bottom: Work out the step number and write it on the hammer. Then write in the missing numbers to complete the sequence.

Name _____ Date _____

Gladiator guesses

● **Estimate two-digit numbers and position them on a number line**

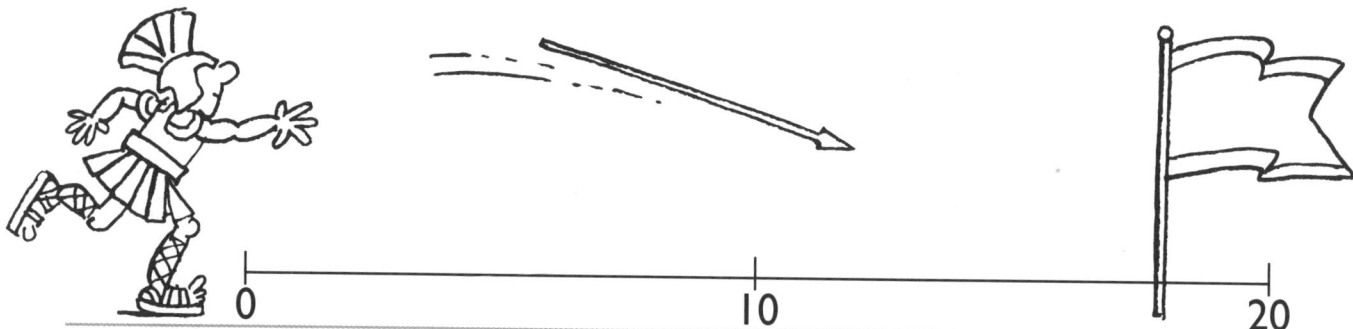

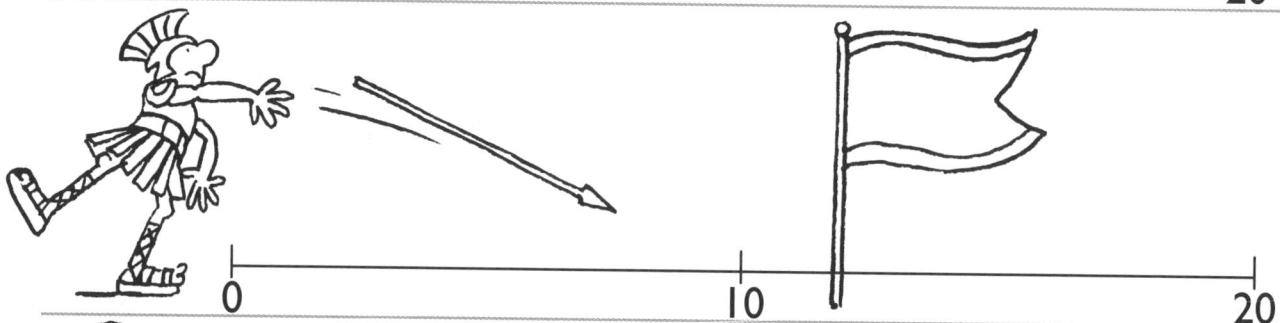

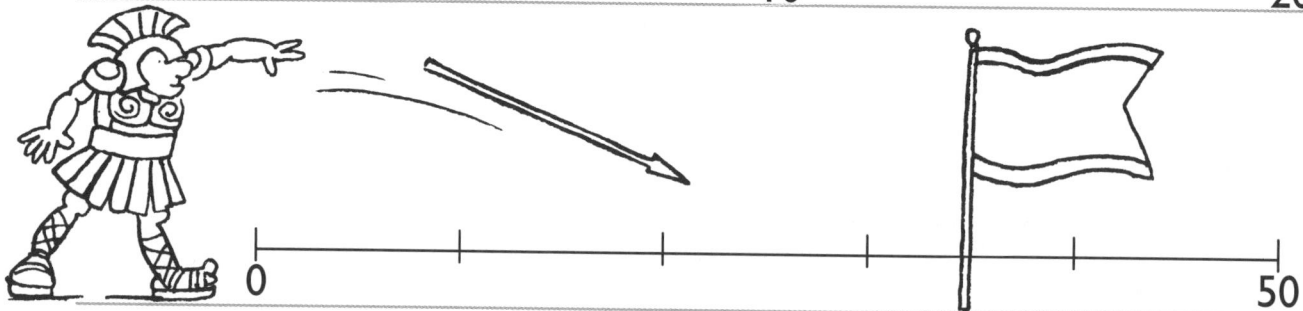

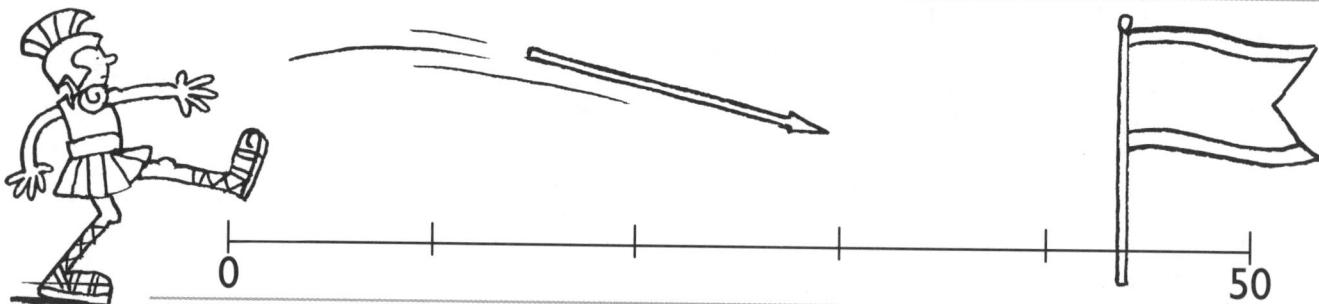

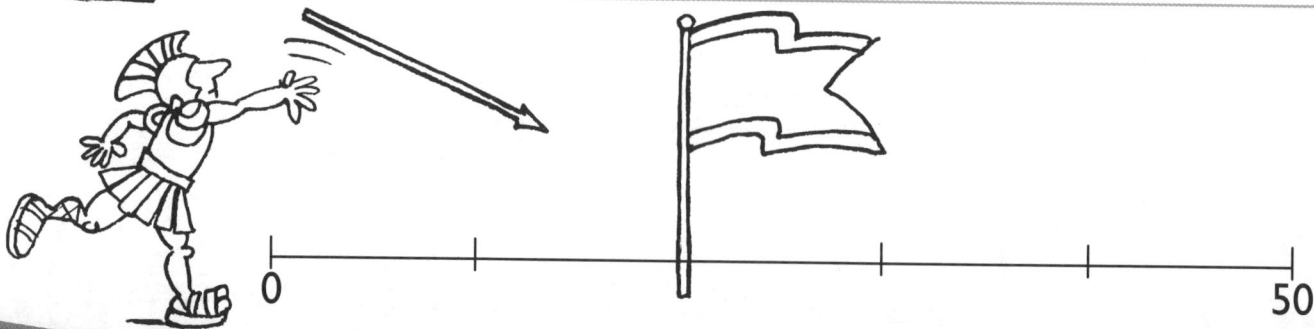

0   10   20

0   10   20

0   50

0   50

0   50

What to do

Estimate how far each gladiator has thrown his javelin along each number line. The flag shows where the javelin will fall. Write your estimate onto the flag.

Name _____ Date _____

Maths machines

● **Understand that subtraction 'undoes' addition**

11

30

7

	+		=	
	−		=	
	−		=	

15

10

14

	+		=	
	−		=	
	−		=	

22

8

16

	+		=	
	−		=	
	−		=	

25

19

6

	+		=	
	−		=	
	−		=	

What to do

Look at each machine. Choose two of the numbers and colour them, writing their total in the space on the machine. Then write the related addition and subtraction calculations as number sentences. Then add them together, writing their total in the box at the end of the machine. Then write the related addition and subtraction calculations.

Name _____ Date _____

Solving squares

● Add 19 or 21 by adding 20 and adjusting by 1

14	(15)	16
	25	

(34)		(36)

15 + 19 = 34

15 + 21 = 36

(24)	25
34	35

◯	◯

_____

_____

35	(36)
45	46

◯	◯

_____

_____

(42)	43
52	53

◯	◯

_____

_____

56	(57)	58

◯	◯

_____

_____

(68)

◯	◯

_____

_____

What to do

Look at these 'pieces' of a 1–100 square. Each one has a number that is circled. Add 19 and 21 to this number to find the missing numbers in the blank circles. Write these numbers into the appropriate spaces, and use them to write the calculations underneath.

On the back: Add 19 and 21 to each of the following numbers: 29, 35, 44, 50. Show how you worked them out.

Name _____ Date _____

Making multiple shapes

● Begin to recognise two-digit multiples of 2, 5 or 10

Colour the multiples of 10.

27 51 100 33
18
62
93 80 90 6
25 94
50 10
45
80 36 1 20
30 70 90 40 60

Name of shape _____

You need:
● coloured pencils

Colour the multiples of 2.

25 43 58 30 24 66
97 64 21 7 90
11 42 65 99 82
16 52 6 78 87
57 43 39

Name of shape _____

Colour the multiples of 5.

48 92 3 83 27
76 55 85 60 35
81 90 13 91 15
54 25 42 64 75
12 40 70 95 100

Name of shape _____

Colour the multiples of 2 and 5.

71 25 99
7 14 22
59 77
15 90
93 89 65
48 11
75 41 27 36
84
31 55 100 63

Name of shape _____

What to do
Colour the multiples as indicated. Write the name of the shape underneath each example.
On the back: Write down ten multiples of 2, 5 and 10 that are larger than 20.

Name _____ Date _____

Camel chains

- Solve mathematical puzzles and recognise simple patterns

Complete the camel chains.

Use the number operations in the tent.
Each number operation can only
be used once.

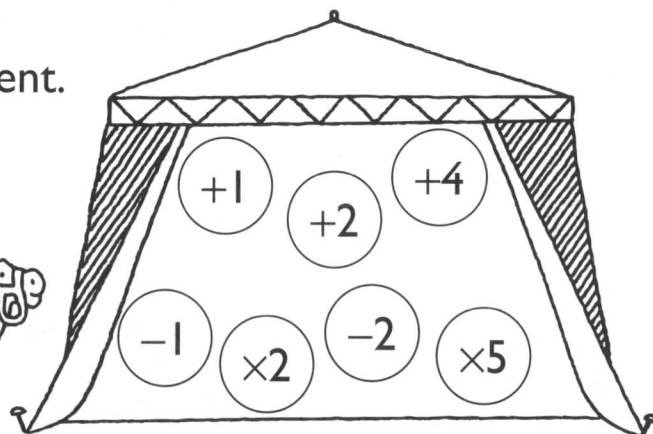

What to do
On the back: Draw ten different chains, beginning with 2 and ending with 12.

Name _____ Date _____

Multiplication magazine

● **Know the 2 and 10 times tables**

How many dinosaurs has Holly got?

Holly has 8 pairs of toy dinosaurs.

How many kittens are there in Asif's home!

Asif has 2 cats. Each cat has 5 kittens.

How many sweets are there altogether?

Tom has 4 cakes. Each cake has 2 sweets on it.

How much does she spend? Each pencil costs 10p.

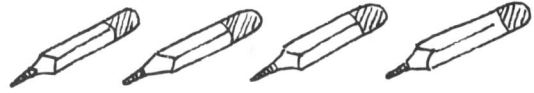

Ella buys 4 pencils.

Multiplication can be done in any order.
Work out each problem, then colour to match answers that are the same.

4 × 10 =	
3 × 2 =	
7 × 10 =	
9 × 2 =	

10 × 7 =	
2 × 9 =	
10 × 4 =	
2 × 3 =	

My Multiplication Magazine

by _____

What to do

Cut along the dotted lines and fold to make a magazine. Complete each multiplication problem.
On the back: Write any other multiplication facts for 2 and 10 that are not shown on this magazine.

Name _____ Date _____

Picnic problems

- **Solve word problems**

Katie made 12 sandwiches. Theo made 8. How many sandwiches altogether?

☐ ◯ ☐ ◯ ☐

The 4 children each had 3 cakes. How many cakes were in the picnic basket?

☐ ◯ ☐ ◯ ☐

They shared the sandwiches with Caie and Lucy. How many did they each have?

☐ ◯ ☐ ◯ ☐

Theo didn't eat his cakes. How many cakes were eaten?

☐ ◯ ☐ ◯ ☐

Lucy brought 15 strawberries and Caie brought 25 strawberries. How many altogether?

☐ ◯ ☐ ◯ ☐

Caie brought 2 packets of biscuits. Each packet had 12 biscuits inside. How many biscuits altogether?

☐ ◯ ☐ ◯ ☐

The 4 children shared the strawberries equally. How many did they each have?

☐ ◯ ☐ ◯ ☐

Katie dropped 4 biscuits before they shared them. How many were left?

☐ ◯ ☐ ◯ ☐

What to do

Read each two-step word problem and complete the number sentences to find the correct answers.
On the back: Look at the last question. How many biscuits did each child have? Now make up a two-step number problem of your own using two different operations. Write and illustrate your problem.

Name _____ Date _____

Lorry loads of shapes

● **Match 3-D solids to their descriptions**

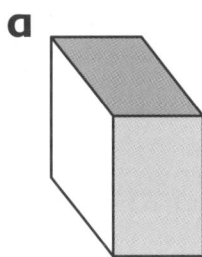

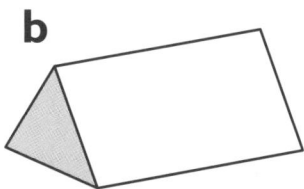

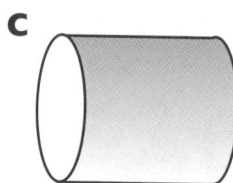

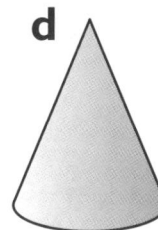

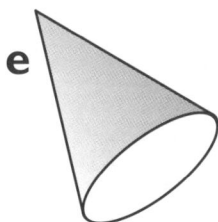

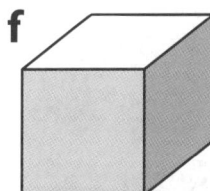

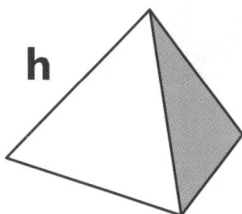

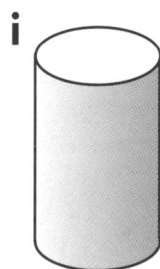

I or more
triangular faces

Curved edges

a

b

c

d

e

f

g

h

i

A shape can be
carried by more
than one lorry.

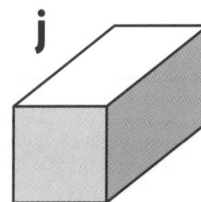

j

8 corners

I or more
rectangular faces

What to do
Look at each 3-D solid. Decide which lorry to load it on to. Write the letter on the lorry.

Name _____ Date _____

Programme times

● Solve problems involving time

News-a-round

start **5:00**

finish **5:15**

Cartoon cavalcade

start **3:45**

finish **4:15**

Cook's corner

start **7:15**

finish **8:00**

Rugby round-up

start **2:30**

finish **4:00**

Film: African adventure

start **3:15**

finish **4:45**

Film: Spaceman

start **7:00**

finish **9:30**

What to do

Look at the clocks. Calculate how long each programme lasts. Write your answer in the box underneath.

Name _____ Date _____

Hunt the litre

● Measure capacity in litres and find out how much other containers hold

These hold less than 1 litre.

1 [jar] of [   ]

2 [bottle] of [   ]

3 [jar] of [   ]

These hold more than 1 litre.

1 [   ] 2 [   ] 3 [   ]

These hold about 1 litre.

1 [   ] 2 [   ] 3 [   ]

What to do

Look at the labels on some bottles, jars and containers. Find three objects which hold less than one litre, three objects which hold more than one litre and three objects with '1 litre' printed on the label. Draw and write the names of these objects in the appropriate places.

Name _____ Date _____

Woodland creatures

● **Sort objects and draw a pictogram**

☐ = 1 creature

Woodland creatures

fox				
squirrel				
owl				
deer				
woodpecker				

Number of creatures

	lives in a tree	does not live in a tree
Can fly	◯	◯
Cannot fly	◯	◯

There are ☐ deer. ☐ creatures live in a tree and can fly.

What to do
Choose a picture to stand for one creature. Draw one picture in the pictogram for each creature. Make a tick for each animal in the sorting sets below. Count the ticks and write the totals in the circles. Complete the sentences.

Name _____ Date _____

Fruit tree block graphs

● Make block graphs

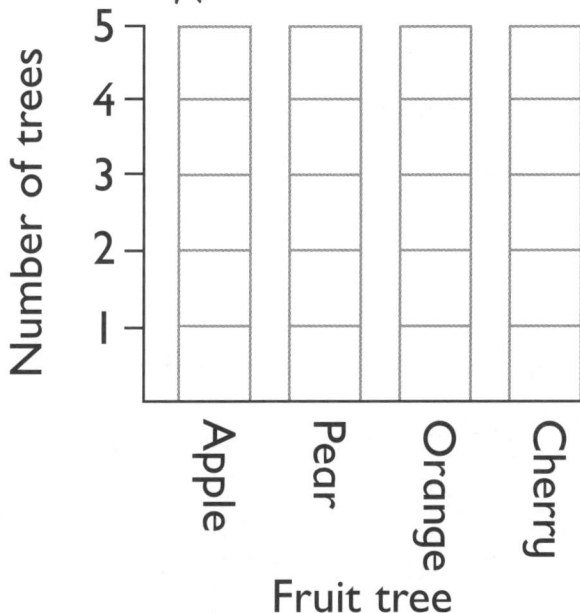

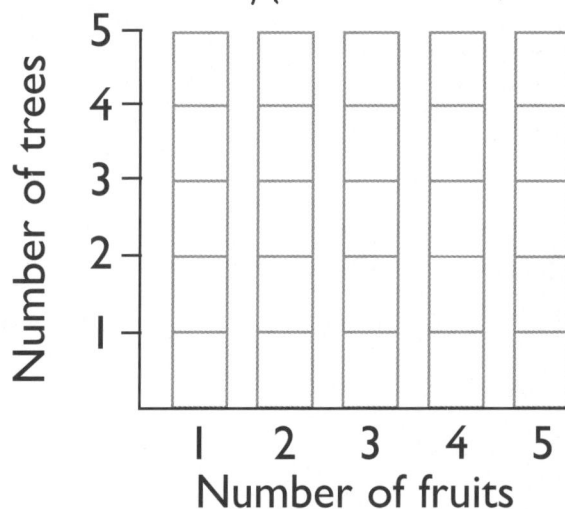

Number of trees

5
4
3
2
1

Apple | Pear | Orange | Cherry

Fruit tree

Number of trees

5
4
3
2
1

1 2 3 4 5

Number of fruits

There are ☐ pear trees.

There are ☐ apple trees.

There are ☐ more orange than cherry trees.

The tree with the most fruits is

☐ trees have 4 fruits.

☐ trees have 5 fruits.

3 trees have ☐ fruits.

You need:

● coloured pencils

What to do

Count the different fruit trees and the number of fruits on them. Colour in the correct number of squares on the block graphs. Complete the sentences under the graphs.

Name _____ Date _____

Front door diagrams

- **Make tables, pictograms and block graphs**

Count the door patterns.

Fill in the table.

Pattern	Number
stripes	
zig-zags	
spots	
squares	

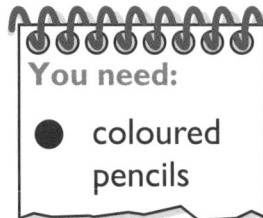

You need:
- coloured pencils

Count the door numbers.

Fill in the table.

Door Number	Number of doors
22	
23	
24	
25	

Make a block graph.

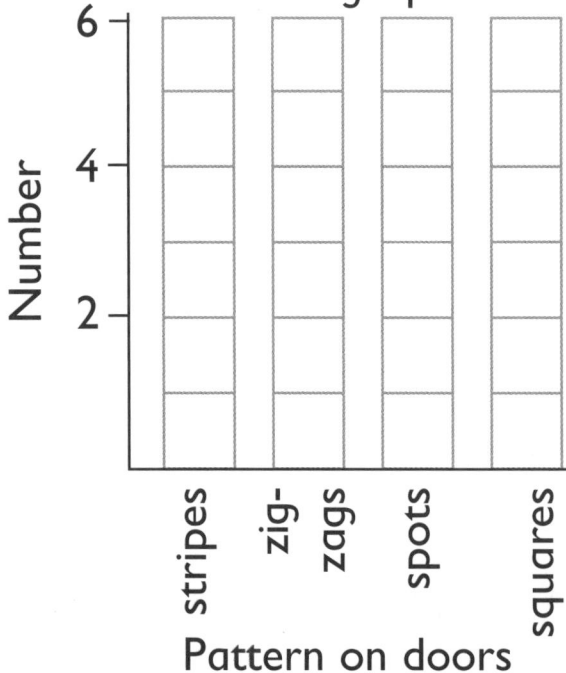

Number

6

4

2

stripes | zig-zags | spots | squares

Pattern on doors

Make a pictogram.

☐ = 1 door

Numbers on doors

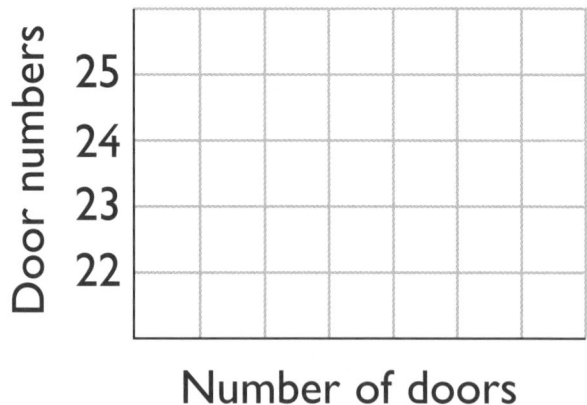

Door numbers

25
24
23
22

Number of doors

There are ☐ doors with stripes.   There is ☐ door numbered 23.

What to do
Read through the sentences and complete the tables, block graph and pictogram.

Name _____ Date _____

Speedy subtraction and addition

● **Add or subtract mentally**

17 + 9 = ☐

18 + 7 = ☐

21 + 7 = ☐

25 − 9 = ☐

16 + 6 = ☐

23 − 8 = ☐

0 1 2 3 4 5 6 7 8 9 10 11 12 13 14 15 16 17 18 19 20 21 22 23 24 25 26 27 28 29 30

What to do
Work with a grown up and use a timer. Individually, complete the addition and subtraction calculations, within a given time. Check the answers together, using a number line.

Name _____ Date _____

Paint pot patterns

● **Recognise patterns in calculations**

2 + 4 = 6

12 + 4 = ☐

22 + 4 = ☐

32 + 4 = ☐

17 − 5 = 12

27 − 5 = ☐

37 − 5 = ☐

47 − 5 = ☐

39 − 8 = 31

49 − 8 = ☐

59 − 8 = ☐

69 − 8 = ☐

47 + 2 = ☐

57 + 2 = 59

67 + 2 = ☐

77 + 2 = ☐

You need:
● scissors
● glue

| 22 | 61 | 69 | 16 | 51 | 32 |
| 49 | 36 | 26 | 41 | 42 | 79 |

What to do
Look at each set of paint pots arranged in rows. Identify the pattern and cut the answers from the bottom of the sheet, sticking them into the correct space.

On the back: Write the pattern for each of these calculations, continuing up to the 90s: 7 + 2 = ☐ and 9 − 5 = ☐.

Name _____ Date _____

Landing times

● Solve problems involving time

landed
15 minutes
early

4:15   6:45   10:15   1:00

landed
15 minutes
late

6:00   6:15   4:45   3:30

What to do

Add or subtract the 15 minutes on each control tower to or from the time shown on each truck. Find the aircraft that
has the answer and colour the truck and aircraft to match.

Name _____ Date _____

Quarter turn patterns

● Know that a right angle is a measure of a quarter turn

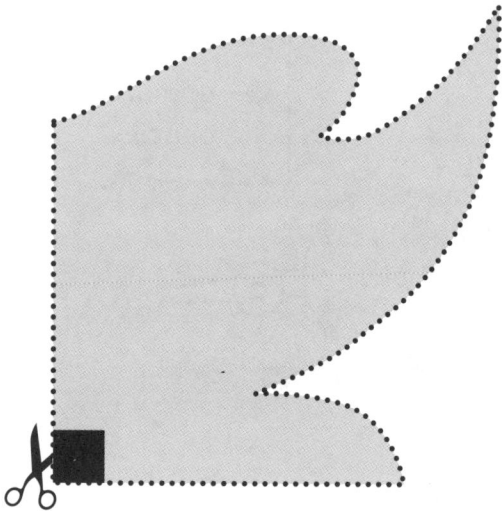

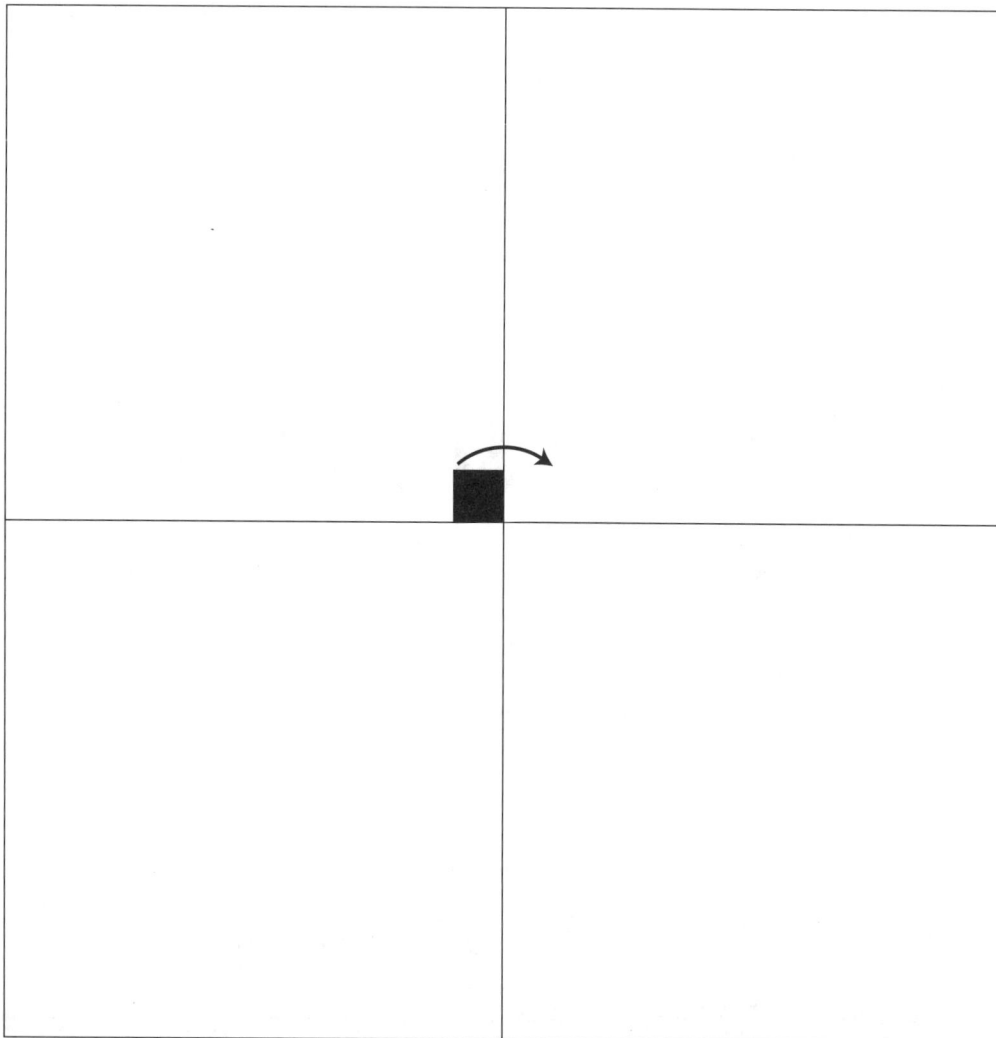

You need:
● scissors
● glue
● card
● coloured
pencils

What to do

Cut out the shape at the top of the sheet. Find a piece of card and stick the shape on to the card. Cut round the shape. Put the right-angled corner of the shape on top of the marked corner in the large square. Make a pattern by drawing round the shape. Turn the card through a quarter turn each time.

Name _____ Date _____

Multiply by 2, 5 and 10

- ● Know the 2, 5 and 10 times tables and the related division facts
- ● Recognise multiples of 2, 5 and 10

7 × 5 =

☐ ÷ ☐ = ☐

14

7 × 2 =

☐ ÷ ☐ = ☐

16

9 × 10 =

☐ ÷ ☐ = ☐

35

10 × 5 =

☐ ÷ ☐ = ☐

90

8 × 2 =

☐ ÷ ☐ = ☐

50

10 × 3 =

30

You need:
- ● scissors
- ● glue

What to do

Cut the numbers from the side of the sheet. Complete each multiplication fact for 2, 5 or 10 by sticking the missing number into each space. Follow the trail and write the related division calculation on to the goal.

Name _____ Date _____

Double quick doubles

● **Know doubles of all numbers to 20**

$1 \times 2 =$ 　　　　　　$4 \times 2 =$

$10 \times 2 =$ 　　　　　$11 \times 2 =$

$7 \times 2 =$ 　　　　　　$18 \times 2 =$

$16 \times 2 =$ 　　　　　$2 \times 2 =$

$3 \times 2 =$ 　　　　　　$19 \times 2 =$

$17 \times 2 =$ 　　　　　$14 \times 2 =$

$9 \times 2 =$ 　　　　　　$8 \times 2 =$

$5 \times 2 =$ 　　　　　　$6 \times 2 =$

$12 \times 2 =$ 　　　　　$13 \times 2 =$

$20 \times 2 =$ 　　　　　$15 \times 2 =$

What to do
Find the doubles for all numbers from 1 to 20, writing the correct numbers into the spaces.
On the back: Choose 10 of these doubles and write each as a division calculation.

Name _____ Date _____

Multiplication and division

● Use arrays to understand multiplication and division

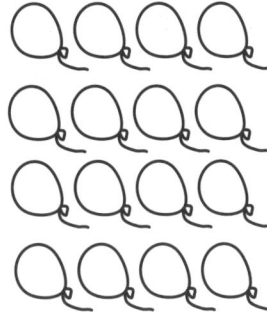

You need:
● scissors
● glue

☐ × ☐ = ☐   ☐ × ☐ = ☐

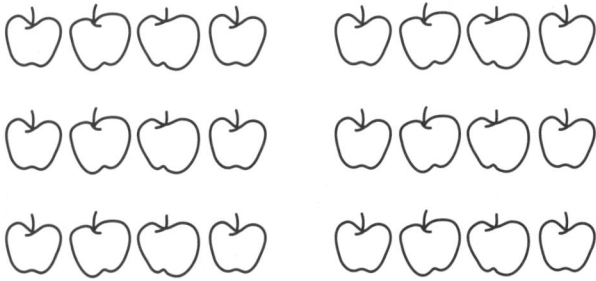

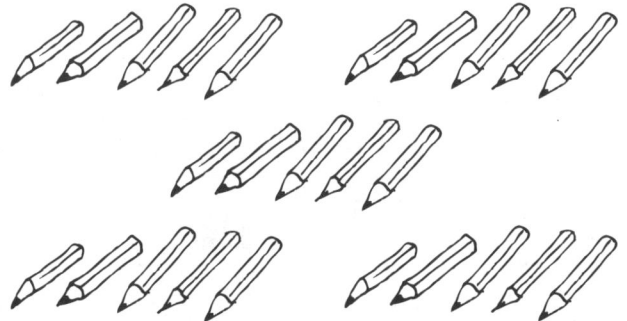

☐ × ☐ = ☐   ☐ × ☐ = ☐

18	÷	3	=	☐		24	÷	6	=	☐

25	÷	5	=	☐		20	÷	5	=	☐

What to do

Cut out the calculations from the bottom of the sheet. Look at each arrangement of objects and stick the most appropriate calculation underneath each one. Write a related multiplication calculation for each arrangement of objects.

Name _____ Date _____

Seaside solutions

- **Solve word problems**

There are 4 sandcastles in a row. Each sandcastle has 3 flags on it. How many flags altogether?

☐ ◯ ☐ ◯ ☐

4 flocks of seagulls fly past. There are 10 gulls in each flock. How many seagulls fly by?

☐ ◯ ☐ ◯ ☐

32 people are on the roller coaster. There are 8 cars joined together. How many people are in each one?

☐ ◯ ☐ ◯ ☐

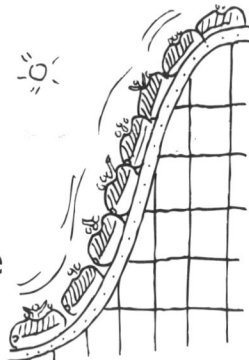

50 people are on the merry-go-round. There are 25 horses to sit on. How many people sit on each horse?

☐ ◯ ☐ ◯ ☐

There are 5 buckets of shells. Each bucket has 10 shells inside. How many shells altogether?

☐ ◯ ☐ ◯ ☐

There are 80 sticks of rock in a sweet shop. There are 4 different flavours. How many sticks of each flavour are there?

☐ ◯ ☐ ◯ ☐

What to do

Look at the word problems, completing each as appropriate.
On the back: Write 2 more seaside problems, one division and one multiplication.

Name _____ Date _____

Party problems

● **Solve word problems**

Six children can sit at one table. There are 22 children. How many tables are needed to seat all the children?

There are 3 jugs of juice. Each jug fills 12 cups. How many cupfuls of juice will there be altogether?

One packet of biscuits contains 5 biscuits. There are 14 children who would like a biscuit. How many packets are needed?

There are 14 jam doughnuts and 15 ring doughnuts. Are there enough doughnuts for all 22 children? If everyone has one each, how many are left?

What to do

Read each word problem and decide which operation to use to find the answer. You can use jottings and drawings to help you to work them out and then write the calculations underneath.

On the back: Write your own word problems, using +, −, x and ÷, one problem for each operation.

Name _____ Date _____

Fraction quiz

● **Find one half, one quarter and three quarters of shapes and sets of objects**

$\frac{1}{4}$

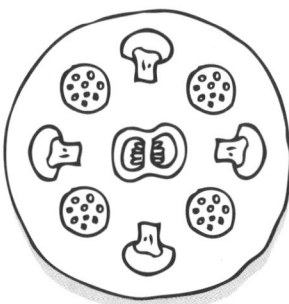

$\frac{3}{4}$

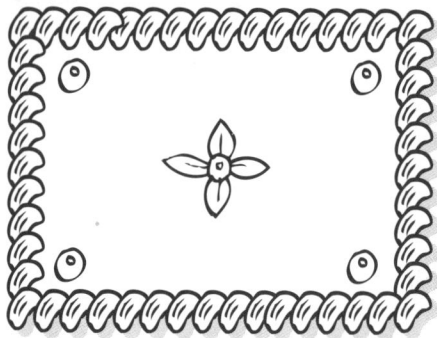

$\frac{1}{2}$

$\frac{2}{4}$

one quarter

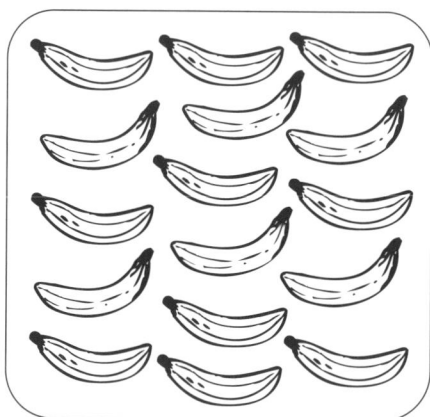

one half

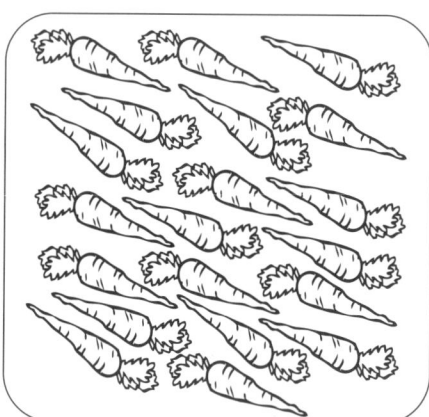

$\frac{3}{4}$

$\frac{1}{2}$

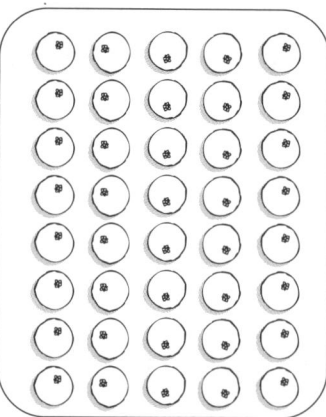

two quarters

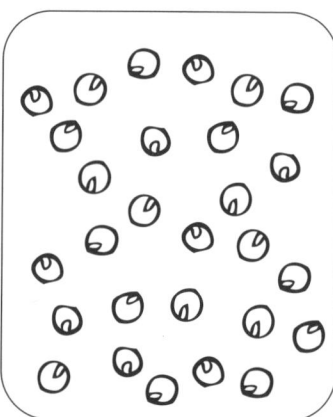

three quarters

You need:

● coloured pencils

What to do

In each row, colour each shape or set of objects according to the fraction indicated. *On the back:* Ask an adult to tell you five multiples of 4 numbers between 0 and 50 and write them down. Find half of each number and write this next to it. Then find $\frac{1}{4}$ and $\frac{3}{4}$ of each number.